Youth Work Policies in England 2019–2023

Bernard Davies

# Youth Work Policies in England 2019–2023

Can Open Youth Work Survive?

Bernard Davies
Leamington Spa, UK

ISBN 978-3-031-65635-4     ISBN 978-3-031-65636-1   (eBook)
https://doi.org/10.1007/978-3-031-65636-1

Cover illustration: Pattern © Harvey Loake

This Palgrave Macmillan imprint is published by the registered company Springer Nature Switzerland AG.
The registered company address is: Gewerbestrasse 11, 6330 Cham, Switzerland

If disposing of this product, please recycle the paper.

# PREFACE

UPDATING AND CONTEXTUALISING

## Filling the Policy Gaps

By mid-2019—that is, less than a year after I had completed *Austerity, Youth Policy and the Deconstruction of the Youth Service in England*[1]—I was having to acknowledge that the book had already '... been overtaken ... by new facts on the ground, shifting ideas and priorities, reconsidered analysis, revised perceptions and interpretations'.[2] This prompted me to start a 'Living History' blog whose stated aim was to explore and comment on current and emerging developments affecting local Youth Services and their provision of 'open youth work'. The posts which followed focused on budget cuts and MP reports, Covid-19 impacts on young people, the role of the National Citizens Service (NCS) and of 'youth voice' and whether (or not) we needed a youth work curriculum.

However, with each topic treated in a largely stand-alone way, it had become clear by mid-2022 that there were significant limitations to this approach—in relation, for example, to how the topics covered were interlinked and their location within a continuously evolving wider policy

---

[1] Bernard Davies, 2019, *Austerity, Youth Policy and the Deconstruction of the Youth Service in England*, Palgrave Macmillan.

[2] Bernard Davies, 2019, 'Living History – Youth Work (De)construction – Updated, July, https://indefenceofyouthwork.com/2019/07/07/bernard-davies-launches-his-blog--youth-works-living-history/, accessed 22 January 2024.

context. This book seeks to address those limitations by, for the five years to December 2023, providing a detailed document of record and commentary on policy developments relevant to 'the youth work sector' in England and to open youth work specifically.

## Defining 'Open Youth Work'

The book, however, has another high-priority aim: to give an explicit profile to the concept of *open* youth work and what distinguishes this from other youth practices. As set out in more detail in my *Youth Work: A Manifesto Revisited*,[3] this distinctiveness assumes a number of crucial bottom lines:

- That open youth work provision and its face-to-face practice are shaped in crucial ways by young people's voluntary participation—by their choice to become involved.
- That key starting points for the practice are identifying and then responding to the interests and concerns of the young people who actually engage.
- That, as an educational practice, it will seek to prompt and help young people to tap more fully and creatively into their potential.
- That, to do this, it will give high priority to building trusting individual and peer group relationships with these young people, particularly via careful negotiation of the inter-personal processes generated by the practice.
- That it will seek to tip balances of power in the young people's favour, both within the youth work practice itself and more widely.
- That it will focus on how young people feel as well as on what they know and can do.

## Key Chapter Focuses

To analyse and evidence the development of open youth work practice and its wider policy contexts in the five years covered by the book, chapters focus on:

---

[3] *Youth and Policy*, 1 October 2021, available at https://www.youthandpolicy.org/articles/youth-work-manifesto-revisited-2021/.

- The continuing influence on government policy-making in this period of neo-liberal thinking and priorities.
- The condition of 'youth'—both overall and in relation to more specific issues affecting their day-to-day lives, including their mental health.
- Funding for open youth work—both during and beyond the post-2010 'austerity decade'.
- How, within and beyond these state policy and funding boundaries, open youth work negotiated its role and contribution.
- The development and implementation of forms of 'youth work' which, redefined, stepped outside the distinctive open youth work model.
- The voluntary youth sector—both 'traditional' and new.
- The role and impacts of the National Youth Agency (NYA).
- Routes to training and qualifying as a youth worker.

With, by early 2024, another period of 'austerity' seeming likely—certain?—a brief 'Epilogue' specifically addresses the question posed in the book's sub-title: Can open youth work survive?

Leamington Spa, UK                                    Bernard Davies

# CONTENTS

# Abbreviations

A&E      Accident and Emergency
APPG      All Party Parliamentary Group
BYC      British Youth Council
CAMHS      Child and Adolescent Mental Health Services
COSMOS      Covid Social Mobility and Opportunities Study
CSJ      Centre for Social Justice
CYI      Centre for Youth Impact
CYPN      *Children and Young People Now*
DCMS      Department of Digital, Media, Culture and Sport
DfE      Department for Education
DMU      De Montfort University
DoE      Duke of Edinburgh Award Scheme
DWP      Department for Work and Pensions
EHC      Educational, Health and Care
EPI      Education Policy Institute
ETS      Education and Training Sub-committee
GCSE      General Certificate of Education
GPs      General Practitioners
IFS      Institute of Fiscal Studies
IMF      International Monetary Fund
JNC      Joint Negotiating Committee
LEAs      Local Education Authorities
LGA      Local Government Association
NAO      National Audit Office
NATCEN      National Centre for Social Research
NCS      National Citizens Service
NCVO      National Council for Voluntary Organisations

| NCVYS | National Council for Voluntary Youth Services |
| NEET | Not in Education, Employment or Training |
| NHS | National Health Service |
| NOS | National Occupational Standards |
| NSPCC | National Society for the Prevention of Cruelty to Children |
| NYA | National Youth Agency |
| NYSAB | National Youth Sector Advisory Board |
| OBR | Office for Budget Responsibility |
| OECD | Office for Economic Co-operation and Development |
| OFSTED | Office for Standards in Education, Children's Services and Skills |
| Ofqual | Office of Qualifications and Examinations Regulation |
| ONS | Office for National Statistics |
| PAC | Peer Action Collective |
| PALYCW | Professional Association of Youth and Community Workers |
| SEND | Special Educational Needs and Disability |
| UNICEF | United Nations International Children's Emergency Fund |
| VCS | Voluntary and Community Sector |
| VRU | Violence Reduction Unit |
| YFF | Young Futures Foundation |
| YIF | Youth Investment Fund |
| YMCA | Young Men's Christian Association |

# CHAPTER 1

# Underpinning Ideology

**Abstract** Throughout the period covered by this book, neo-liberal ideas committed to individualistic, competitive, privatising and anti-state priorities continued to influence government policies, including ones focused on youth services. Though the Covid-19 pandemic initially prompted some critical, largely pragmatic, scrutiny of these ideas, their constraints on these services remained, including on open youth work provision in England. One significant consequence was to raise the profile and extend the role of voluntary youth organisations, both via state commissioning procedures and as direct providers of open youth work facilities previously funded and run by the state.

**Keywords** Neo-liberalism • Anti-state • Covid-19 pandemic • Voluntary youth organisations • Commissioning

## The Neo-liberal Mind-set

Throughout the period covered by this book, Conservative governments remained deeply committed to neo-liberalism's individualistic, competitive, privatising and anti-state priorities. Far from co-incidentally, during these years, the long-standing structural inequalities embedded within the UK continued to deepen. In relation to class, this was, for example, illustrated in early 2022 by the evidence that if wages had risen over the previous two decades at the same rate as company dividends, they would have been £2100 a year or 8 per cent higher.[1] Evidence also accumulated on inequalities linked to gender and race.[2]

For youth work, one particularly significant but often unremarked consequence of these neo-liberal influences was philanthropy's increasing presentation—by government and often, too, by voluntary organisations themselves—as a credible alternative funder and provider of those public services. Historically, of course, the role of these organisations in the UK had been crucial in creating, complementing and extending this provision, particularly when, bottom-up, it had emerged out of users' direct experience and action. It had also often imposed fewer of the bureaucratic procedures which over the years came to constrain much state-funded provision, including that of open youth work (see Chap. 4).

Embedded within the more top-down philanthropic processes, however, there have been (and often still are) at least implicit judgements by the wealthy, the privileged and the powerful on who are deserving of their support—and, at least by implication, who are not.[3] By thus in effect de-politicising what are at root crucial political issues, philanthropy's growing influence contributed to the period's 'retreat from the state'[4] and in particular from services paid for *as a citizen's right* out of the public purse. As, for example, Mae Shaw pointed out very early in the Covid-19 pandemic:

> *In the midst of such sincere outpouring of public goodwill, it can seem churlish to remind people that the British National Health Service is a tax-funded public service, not a charity ....*[5]

Though that was once true, too, of a significant proportion of open access youth work provision—both building-based and outreach/detached—in October 2022, the National Youth Agency's (NYA's) annual

[1] Richard Partington, 2022, 'Rate of UK dividend growth outstripping wage increases, says report', *Guardian*, 2 May.

[2] Prince's Trust/NatWest Group, 2022, *The Prince's Trust NatWest Youth Index 2022*, Prince's Trust, February, https://www.princes-trust.org.uk/about-the-trust/news-views/princes-trust-natwest-youth-index-2022.

[3] See, for example, Polly Toynbee, 2023, *An Uneasy Inheritance: My Family and Other Radicals*, Atlantic Books, pp. 85–6.

[4] Polly Toynbee, 2022, 'The Return of the State by Graeme Garrard review – why big government is back', *Guardian*, 7 May.

[5] Mae Shaw, 2020, 'Editorial', *Concept*, available at http://concept.lib.ed.ac.uk/article/view/4364/5954.

National Youth Sector Census revealed that youth charities and community groups were 'disproportionally providing', and being commissioned by local authorities to provide, open access and out-of-school activities for young people.[6] By the following September, however, a fifth of over 750 youth work providers consulted by NYA had waiting lists of between three and six months, a quarter had less than six months' worth of reserves and those operating in the most deprived areas were finding it difficult to recruit volunteers.[7]

## NEO-LIBERALISM UNDER SCRUTINY

After the 2016 Brexit referendum had for some produced the 'wrong' result, a somewhat more critical debate on neo-liberalism did open up, including amongst some in powerful financial and policy-making roles. In December 2016, for example, the then Governor of the Bank of England, Mark Carney, acknowledged that

> ... *many citizens in advanced economies are facing heightened uncertainty ... and losing trust in the system ... Rather than a new golden age, globalisation is associated with low wages, insecure employment, stateless corporations and striking inequalities.*[8]

Three years later, the then head of the International Monetary Fund (IMF), Christine Lagarde, noted that 'there are more members (of the Fund) concerned about inequality—which is excessive in many areas of the world—and how to remedy it ...'.[9] Questioning the neo-liberal power structures from within became even sharper in the UK in the autumn of 2022 when Prime Minister Liz Truss's ruthless tax-cutting 'programme

---

[6] NYA, 2022, *Delivering youth work in England: National Youth Sector Census, Second Report*, NYA, October; Nicole Weinstein, 2022, 'Councils turn to charities to deliver open access youth work, *Children and Young People Now (CYPN)*, 31 October.

[7] Emily Harle, 2023, 'Youth work waiting lists soar amid financial pressures, report finds', *CYPN*, 18 September.

[8] Katie Allen, 2016, 'Mark Carney: we must tackle isolation and detachment caused by globalisation', *Guardian*, 6 December.

[9] Larry Elliott, 2019, 'Nations must protect spending on the vulnerable, says IMF chief' *Guardian*, 14 June.

for government' threw the global financial system into panic and created an ongoing budget crisis within the UK itself.[10]

By then, the arrival of Covid-19 had anyway prompted a serious challenge to some of these free-market positions, resulting in acknowledgements that, for example, 'the state (is) no enemy of enterprise but its only salvation' and that 'there is no substitute for big government'.[11] As the pandemic further exposed and indeed exacerbated economic inequalities, even hard-line monetarists had to face the reality that, if disaster (economic as well as social) was to be avoided, then only 'the state'—even in the form of the Bank of England—had the power and resources to respond effectively.

Between February 2020 and July 2021, for example, Chancellor of the Exchequer Rishi Sunak—a dedicated monetarist ideologue—found £370 billion of public money to ameliorate the pandemic's worst impacts[12] while private companies long suspicious of the state intervening in their activities suddenly found themselves calling for it to give them more financial support.[13] As the cost-of-living crisis began to take hold, during her 44 days in power, even Liz Truss found herself having to promise some state-funded financial support for people unable to keep their homes heated during winter.[14]

Most of these responses, however, were largely pragmatic—propelled by circumstances rather than by a change in the underlying ideology. For many other government interventions—most noticeably its Covid track, trace and test programmes—the bottom line remained that only the private sector was capable of delivering what was needed. However, not only did the procedures for awarding contracts often fail to achieve their main

---

[10] See, for example, Larry Elliott and Rowena Mason, 2022, 'A budget for the rich', *Guardian*, 24 September.

[11] Polly Toynbee, 2022, 'The Return of the State by Graeme Gerrard review – why big government is back', *Guardian*, 7 May.

[12] Adam Tooze, 2021, 'The Guardian view on pro-market thinking: ministers want it to survive Covid', *Guardian*, 21 October.

[13] See, for example, BBC News, 2021, 'Covid: Business alarmed at prospect of further restrictions', 19 December, https://www.bbc.co.uk/news/business-59700289; Joanna Partridge and Sarah Butler, 2021, '"Knife edge": Nightclub ad gym owners call for urgent financial help', *Guardian*, 21 December.

[14] BBC, 2022, 'Liz Truss reveals plans for tackling rising energy bills', https://www.bbc.co.uk/newsround/62833717.

objective.[15] They could even turn out to be dangerously ineffective[16] and at times bordered on the corrupt and the illegal.[17] At one point, it also emerged that some consultancy firms—many long-standing donors to the Conservative Party[18]—were being paid £1 million a day, with some individual consultants getting more than £6000 for a day's work.[19] All at a time when that core state provider in the field, the National Health Service (NHS), at great speed and with great effectiveness, was delivering a huge and hugely successful vaccination programme.

Nonetheless, though voter polling suggested that free-market ideas were 'very much a kind of minority pursuit',[20] for most within influential UK government circles, the commitment to low taxes and small-state privatised services remained unshakable. This was, for example, again exposed during the Conservative Party leadership campaign in the summer of 2022[21] and demonstrated by the Truss budget proposals that followed. Under pressure from a significant and influential group of his backbenchers to cut taxes, it was then sustained by Sunak after he became Prime Minister in October.[22] Even though by then the NHS was in serious financial trouble[23] and local councils across the country were making major cuts

[15] Andrew Gregory, 2021, 'NHS test and trace "failed its main objective", says spending watchdog', *Guardian*, 27 October.

[16] Rowena Mason, 2021, 'Firm that gave 43,000 false Covid results still processing PCR tests', *Guardian*, 26 October.

[17] Good Law Project, 2022, 'We plan to ask the Supreme Court to hear an appeal', https://goodlawproject.org/update/we-plan-to-ask-the-supreme-court-to-hear-an-appeal/?utm_source=NB&utm_campaign=public%20first%20update%20rec%20donors%20210122&utm_medium=email, accessed 22 January 2022.

[18] Rowena Mason, Rob Evans and Joseph Smith, 2021, 'Michael Give Backer won £184m in PPE contracts after "VIP lane" referral', *Guardian*, 16 November.

[19] Hettie O'Brien, 2023, 'From Puerto Rico's bankruptcy to Britain's Covid contracts: the private firms taking over public life', *Guardian*, 16 February.

[20] Peter Walker, 2024, 'Mhairi Fraser the rising Tory force who was bowled over by Trump', *Guardian*, 10 Feb. 24.

[21] See, for example, Richard Partington and Peter Walker, 2022, 'Scale of tax cuts promised by Tory leadership hopefuls may cause "fiscal black hole"', *Guardian*, 13 July.

[22] George Eaton, 2022, 'Rishi Sunak isn't a centrist technocrat – he's a proud Thatcherite', *New Statesman*, 22 October; Larry Elliott, 2024, 'IMF warns Jeremy Hunt against tax cuts in budget', *Guardian*, 30 January.

[23] See, for example, Toby Helm and Denis Campbell, 2023, 'NHS sinks into £7bn cash crisis as inflation and strikes bite', *Guardian*, 17 September.

to their services,[24] the result was a Budget in March 2024, one of whose dominant themes was tax cuts.

For open youth work and its actual practice, these dominant neo-liberal policy contexts could have significant consequences—illustrated by the evidence set out in Chap. 5 of how attention and especially resources were diverted to redefined conceptions of 'youth work' with focuses on, for example, youth violence, schooling and employment and mental health.

[24] Jessica Murray, 2023, 'Nottingham city council plans cuts to libraries, care homes and youth services', *Guardian*, 12 December.

# CHAPTER 2

# The Condition of Young People

**Abstract** Young people's situation in the UK has long been shaped by deeply embedded structural factors defined, for example, by class, gender, ethnicity, disability and sexual orientation. Often oversimply labelled 'disadvantages' by state policy-makers, these inequalities have been both further exposed and exacerbated by the Covid pandemic and the cost-of-living crisis. As a result, growing numbers of young people are struggling to attend school, find and keep a job, make ends meet and live independently or avoid homelessness. With their mental health already under pressure pre-Covid, the relevant support services in the period covered by the book have often been unable to cope with the huge extra demands made on them by young people.

**Keywords** Structural inequalities • Covid pandemic • Cost-of-living crisis • Schooling • Jobs • Housing • Mental health

## STRUCTURAL INEQUALITY—THE (LONG) BACKSTORY

Well before Covid-19 arrived, evidence was building that neo-liberal policies had had and were continuing to have damaging impacts on young people's lives. Usually downplayed by government policy-makers as mere 'disadvantages', their underlying causes were often traceable to the embedded structural inequalities outlined in the previous chapter.

© The Author(s), under exclusive license to Springer Nature Switzerland AG 2024
B. Davies, *Youth Work Policies in England 2019-2023*,
https://doi.org/10.1007/978-3-031-65636-1_2

In 2018—that is, a decade after the global banking crisis and well into the austerity decade—journalist John Lanchester had talked of 'a fundamental breach of what used to be the social contract' resulting, he said, in young people's future living standards '… likely not to be as high as they are for their parents'.[1] This view was echoed three years later by Joe Moran, a social historian, who concluded that '(t)he huge growth in private wealth compared to growth in income ensures that advantage and disadvantage will be passed down the generations'.[2] In support, he quoted from a book by the Director of the Policy Institute, Bobby Duffy, sub-titled *Does When You're Born Shape Who You Are?*. This suggested that these inequalities were 'a key reason for people of all ages being more likely to question whether our economic systems are working'.[3] By then, a Sutton Trust study published in 2018 had provided detailed evidence of how parents from higher socioeconomic groups were ensuring that their children gained the fullest advantage from the education system.[4]

Six months later, the government's own Social Mobility Commission tellingly concluded that inequality in Britain was 'now entrenched from birth to work', including within the teenage period, so that 'being born privileged means you are likely to remain privileged …'.[5] Children who had 'professional' parents were thus 80 per cent more likely to go into a professional occupation, while even those from working-class backgrounds who successfully made this journey were still, on average, earning 17 per cent less than colleagues from more privileged backgrounds. A House of Lords Select Committee reached a similar conclusion in 2021—including that 'the action and inaction of successive governments' had risked undermining the relationship between older and younger generations,[6] while according to an Institute for Fiscal Studies (IFS) report published in Sep-

[1] John Lanchester, 2018, 'After the Fall', *London Review of Books*, Vol 40, No 13, 5 July.
[2] Joe Moran, 2023, 'Gen Z and Me', *London Review of Books*, Vol 45, No 4, 16 February.
[3] Quote referenced as: Bobby Duffy, 2021, *Generation: Does When You're Born Shape Who You Are?*, Atlantic.
[4] Rebecca Montacute and Carl Cullinane, 2018, *Parent Power 2018: How parents use financial and cultural resources to boost their children's chances of success'*, Sutton Trust, September.
[5] Richard Adams, 2019, 'Social mobility in UK "virtually stagnant" since 2014', *Guardian*, 30 April.
[6] www.parliament.uk, 2021, *Intergenerational Fairness and Provision Committee Report*, https://lordslibrary.parliament.uk/intergenerational-fairness-and-provision-committee-report/, 21 January. See also Nina Jacobs, 2019, '"BYC backs measures to tackle intergenerational inequality"', *CYPN*, 26 April.

tember 2023, those born into poor households, especially in the north and Midlands and from ethnic minorities, 'may find it harder now that at any point in over half a century to move up …'.[7]

## Covid and Its Impacts

### *Some Positives …*

Even as Covid was adding to these constraints, some more optimistic interpretations of how young people were responding did emerge. While urging caution, in an article in the *Guardian* in June 2021, psychology lecturer Lucy Foulkes referenced a 2020 study which concluded that 'plenty of people navigate the "storm and stress" of these (adolescent) years without any significant emotional cost'. She thus highlighted a need to 'explore and celebrate what makes young people resilient' as well as to pay close attention to those who were struggling.[8]

Nine months later, Almuth McDowall, a psychology professor at the University of London, suggested that some young people were in fact undergoing 'a collective process of fundamental re-evaluation … about what makes their lives good and meaningful'. This, she said, was resulting in some 'significantly different lifestyle decisions to the generations before them'.[9] Nearly three years into the pandemic, Sport England's annual survey generated more grounded findings on this, including, for example, that secondary school girls were more active than they had ever been, with 100,000 more girls playing football than five years before.[10]

Wider evidence of this 're-evaluation' is clearly needed, particularly in relation, for example, to ethnicity, sexual orientation and disability. Nonetheless, insofar as it indicated changes in young people's self-identities and in how they were developing personally and socially, it would seem to have significant potential implications for open-access youth work and how its practitioners might support and contribute to these changes.

---

[7] Richard Partington, 2023, 'UK social mobility at its worst in over 50 years, report finds', *Guardian*, 7 September.

[8] Lucy Foulkes, 2021, 'Covid's "lost generation" may be more resilient than we think', *Guardian*, 2 June.

[9] Amelia Hill, 2022, 'Why millenials like Ash Barty are rethinking work', *CYPN*, 25 March.

[10] Sally Weale, 2022, '100,000 more girls playing football in England as activity levels rebound', *Guardian*, 8 December.

### ... *And the Damage*

However, as many other studies were revealing, the impacts on young people's lives—particularly of the pandemic and the cost-of-living crisis—were often immediate and far from positive. At the end of May 2020, for example—that is, during the first Covid lockdown—the National Youth Agency published *Out of Sight*,[11] a report on the pandemic's consequences for 'vulnerable' young people. After pointing to three groups of 8–19-year-olds particularly in need of safeguarding and support, this raised 'urgent' concerns about the continuing consequences of the lockdown such as—explored in more detail below—the approximately 700,000 young people by then 'missing from education'.

With many seen as 'lacking a "safe" space', the report also highlighted a range of long-standing risks facing young people. These included:

- Being drawn into highly dangerous and exploitative county lines drug activity.
- Becoming 'NEET' (not in education or training).
- Experiencing domestic abuse.
- Joining the nearly half a million young people who were homeless or living in a 'precarious' housing situation.
- Being one of the approximately one million young people estimated to have little or no digital access at home.

A UK Youth report published a year later, in March 2021,[12] also found that some young people didn't have the necessary digital equipment or a suitable environment in which to use it. This was resulting in limited access to relevant services and 'increased engagement in gang activity and anti-social behaviours'. Some of these effects were exacerbated by a 'lack (of) understanding of the Covid-19 guidance and what they are allowed to do' and by a resultant fear of the police and of being fined. Some young people said that in the process they were 'losing self-confidence (and) feeling disconnected and experiencing anxiety'.

One finding from an NYA report published in March 2021 was particularly revealing about open youth work's overall contribution to

---

[11] NYA, 2020, *Out of Sight - Vulnerable Young People: COVID-19 Response*, April, https://www.nya.org.uk/resource/out-of-sight-vulnerable-young-people-covid-19-response/.

[12] UK Youth, 2021, *The Impact of Covid-19 on England's Youth Organisations: Executive Summary*, March, UK-Youth-Fund-Report-Executive-Summary1.pdf.

responses to these kinds of risk: that over 448,000 young people from vulnerable families not known to wider services *were* likely to be known to youth workers.[13]

A report published in May 2020 had focused specifically on the Covid impacts on 'social mobility'.[14] This had revealed how the pandemic 'had exacerbated existing inequalities defined by income, place, health and ethnicity', with the young emerging as one of the groups 'disproportionately affected'.[15] This latter point was again illustrated by a finding published the following September that, though by then infections were decreasing in the older age groups, in England these were still growing fastest amongst 10–29-year-olds.[16]

A year later, a specifically young person perspective was provided by a 'Youth Evidence Review' report commissioned by the Department for Digital, Culture, Media and Sport (DCMS).[17] Based on responses gathered in September 2020 and January 2021 from eight focus groups of 13–24-year-olds located in urban, rural and coastal areas of England, it pointed to a number of issues considered in more detail later in this chapter.

- 'While most young people reported being happy and satisfied with their lives, a proportion … experience dissatisfaction …'. Significantly in the context of a decade of cuts to youth work provision (see Chap. 3), this included 'not having access to friendly and affordable space … (to) build and develop their friendships'.
- 'Some groups … felt unsafe because of their race, religion, sexual orientation or gender identity'.

[13] NYA, Between The Lines', March 2021, p4, https://static.nya.org.uk/static/f3fcc0c77f1f2d3b579af6274648540b/Between-the-lines-final-version.pdf.

[14] Lee Elliot Major and Stephen Machin, 2020, *Covid-19 and social mobility*, Centre for Economic Performance/LSE, May, http://cep.lse.ac.uk/pubs/download/cepcovid-19-004.pdf.

[15] See also for example Denis Campbell, 2020, 'Racism contributed to disproportionate UK BAME coronavirus deaths, inquiry finds', *Guardian*, 14 June.

[16] Niamh McIntyre and Pamela Duncan, 2020, 'Coronavirus cases rise steeply among young people in England', *Guardian*, 7 September.

[17] Hannah Briggs, Martin Mitchell and Emma Forsyth, 2021, *Youth Evidence: Deep dive focus group findings*, NatCent Social Research, 21 March, accessed via https://www.gov.uk/government/publications/youth-evidence-review-part-1-2, for example, pp. 8–9.

- 'Young people across the focus groups thought there was not enough support (or they were unaware of support) available for their mental health …'.
- 'Young people were worried about finding work in the future'.

The report also stressed that '… it was important for young people to be meaningfully involved in decision-making about policies and services which affected them' by being offered 'a choice of ways to engage …'. This was an issue which the Children's Commissioner for England sought specifically to address in September 2023 when she announced that ahead of the next general election, she would be asking young people about their political priorities.[18]

Similar concerns emerged from The Prince's Trust's annual Youth Index survey of over 2100 16–25-year-olds, carried out in December 2021 and January 2022. Giving expression to young people's own downbeat assessment of Covid's continuing impacts, it recorded that some of the biggest drops in their confidence and happiness were in relation to employment, training and qualifications.[19] These same disappointments were reported a year later both again by the Trust and also by a Covid-focused study carried out by the Sutton Trust which attracted 13,000 respondents.[20]

Other research suggested that young people's 'disadvantages' even extended to the help they were getting from charities. In September 2021, for example, 17 per cent of under-25s reported that, compared with just 1 per cent of over-65s, they'd been unable to use the services these offered.[21] This coincided with the release of another enquiry's finding that nearly half of the UK adults who responded '… leant towards thinking of young people as having been selfish during the pandemic'. Not only was this rejected by a number of the young people interviewed,[22] but it was

[18] Emily Harle, 2023, 'Children's commissioner seeks young people's views ahead of the general election', *CYPN*, 14 September.

[19] Prince's Trust/NatWest Group, 2022, *The Prince's Trust NatWest Youth Index 2022*, Princes Trust, February, https://www.princes-trust.org.uk/about-the-trust/news-views/princes-trust-natwest-youth-index-2022.

[20] Amelia Hill, 2023, '"Debilitating" effects of the pandemic linger for Britain's young', *Guardian*, 30 January.

[21] Joe Lepper, 2021, 'Young people worst hit by charity cuts' *CYPN*, 30 September.

[22] King's College London News Centre, 2021, 'Young people seen as selfish rather than selfless during Covid (including by themselves)', 18 September, https://www.kcl.ac.uk/news/young-people-seen-as-selfish-rather-than-selfless-during-covid-including-by-themselves; Rachel Obordo and Mattha Busby, 2020, 'Don't blame us for UK's coronavirus spike, say young people', *Guardian*, 8 September.

explicitly contradicted by evidence from other research referenced earlier—that, in order to protect parents and grandparents, young people's Covid lockdown compliance had remained high.[23]

Once the official Covid Inquiry into the handling of the pandemic got under way, it also became clear that there had been serious systemic failings in the government's approach to safeguarding and supporting children and young people. At an early session in November 2023, the barrister representing three children's organisations suggested, for example, that the young had been disproportionately affected by pandemic policies because, with their voices not listened to, they were 'at the back of the queue when the government made its biggest decisions about lockdown and reopening the economy'.[24]

## LIFE DAY-TO-DAY

### *Making Ends Meet in a Cost-of-Living Crisis*

Though often hidden within the label 'children',[25] many in their teens and twenties had long been located in what had come to be recognised as a new 'precariat'.[26] The government's own Household Income Data, for example, showed that in 2016–17, for the third year running, the numbers in these age groups living in poverty relative to other age groups in the population had increased to its highest level since 2007–08.[27] Six months later, the Social Metrics Commission's updated measure of poverty put this total at 4.5 million, with more than half seen as likely to remain trapped in that situation for years.[28]

---

[23] Joe Moran, 2023, 'Gen Z and Me', *London Review of Books*, Vol 45, No 4,16 February.

[24] Andy Hillier, 2023, 'Children were failed by pandemic policies, Covid Inquiry told', *Guardian*, 4 October.

[25] See, for example, Brigid Francis-Devine et al, 2019, 'Poverty in the UK: Statistics', Briefing paper 7096, House of Commons Library, 2 July which defined 'children' as '… aged under 16, or who are aged 16–19, not married or co-habiting and in full-time non-advanced education'.

[26] See, for example, Martin Allen, 2021, *Why young people can't get the jobs they want and the education they need*, Radicaled Books, 2nd edition, May, https://radicaled.files.wordpress.com/2021/12/why-young-people-cant-get-the-jobs-they-want.pdf, p. 14.

[27] Tristan Donovan, 2018A, '"Child poverty hits highest level in decade"', *CYPN*, 22 March.

[28] Patrick Butler, 2018, 'New study finds 4.5 million UK children living in poverty', *Guardian*, 17 September.

Compelling evidence came, too, from a non-UK source—the United Nations 'rapporteur' on extreme poverty, Philip Alston. Drawing on a two-week fact-finding tour in November 2018, his final report released in May 2019 called the situation in twenty-first-century Britain a 'social calamity'. In response to almost one in two children being poor, he, for example, described the Department for Work and Pensions (DWP) as seemingly having been 'tasked with designing a digital and sanitised version of the nineteenth century workhouse'.[29]

Driven by large increases in fuel prices, tax rises, a below-inflation increase in benefit payments and, for many in their 20s, proposed higher interest rates on loans to students in higher education,[30] 'the cost of living crisis' added to young people's financial struggles. Early impacts on them were illustrated in reports from Centrepoint and the Young Men's Christian Association (YMCA), both published in the summer of 2021. These revealed that, with the Chancellor's temporary uplift to the benefit system's universal credit allowance due to end in September, the resultant weekly cut of 25.2 per cent to the standard allowance would 'disproportionately' affect some one million under-25-year-old claimants already on a lower rate than over 25s.[31] Unsurprisingly perhaps therefore, by January 2022, some 23 per cent of this age group were expressing doubts about whether they would ever be financially secure—a figure rising to 43 per cent amongst those who were NEET.[32]

With a range of underlying factors identified as having their effects, within all of this, a gender pay gap had left 18–30-year-old women each year earning a fifth—£5080—less on average than a man of the same age.[33]

---

[29] UN General Assembly, 2019, 'Visit to the United Kingdom of Great Britain and Northern Ireland: Report of the Special Rapporteur on extreme poverty and human rights', June-July, paras 3, 13, accessed at https://digitallibrary.un.org/record/3806308?ln=en#record-files-collapse-headerA_HRC_41_39_Add-1-EN.pdf.

[30] Kimi Chaddah, 2022, 'Under-30s pay the highest price for the UK's cost-of-living crisis', *Guardian*, 21 March; Richard Adams, 2022, 'IFS: England's student loan change to hit poor and minority ethnic people hardest', *Guardian*, 27 April.

[31] Joe Lepper, 2021, 'Young people to be "hit hardest" by the end of universal credit uplift', *CYPN*, 11 August; Joe Lepper, 2021, 'Almost 1 million young people to be hit by universal credit cut', *CYPN*, 15 September.

[32] Kate Ng, 2022, 'A quarter of young people don't think they will ever feel financial secure', *Independent*, 6 January.

[33] Young Women's Trust, 2023, 'The Income Gap: the scale and causes of pay inequality for young women in the UK', 21 June, https://www.youngwomenstrust.org/our-research/the-income-gap/.

This, the Young Women's Trust reported in September 2023, was resulting in young women

> ... *trapped in jobs where they were miserable, discriminated against, or even unsafe because they can't afford to move. They're losing hope and their talents are going to waste.*[34]

By March 2022, with the median gross weekly wage of 18–21-year-olds having fallen in real terms since 1997 by almost a fifth, another Centrepoint report revealed that in the previous 12 months, almost half of the two thousand 16–25-year-olds surveyed had been forced to go to bed hungry and that 35 per cent had gone a whole day without food.[35] A review of support services for the under-25s in Leicester, Leicestershire and Rutland published six months later produced similar evidence, particularly on young parents' struggles to feed themselves and their children.[36] By mid- to late 2023, this was being placed in a wider national context by reports from Buttle UK, a charity providing financial grants to children in need, and the Joseph Rowntree Foundation. These talked of a 'significant increase' in child destitution over the previous two years and of over one million children whose families could not afford to adequately feed, clothe or clean them or keep them warm.[37]

By then (November 2022), the market research company YouGov had released findings which identified significant generational gaps—such as that, compared with only 3 per cent of over 65s, 26 per cent of 18–24-year-olds reported having to borrow money to pay for food.[38] Two months later, a Young Minds study concluded that money worries were a key

[34] Young Women's Trust, 2023, 'Why are young women worse affected by the cost of living crisis?', 27 September, https://www.youngwomenstrust.org/our-research/our-new-research-shows-the-cost-of-living-crisis-is-hitting-young-women-harder/#:~:text=Key%20findings,women's%20has%20got%20substantially%20worse.

[35] Fiona Simpson, 2022, 'Half of young people skipping meals as cost of living increases, Centrepoint finds', *CYPN*, 21 July.

[36] Fiona Simpson, 2022, 'Cost-of-living crisis has "significant" impact on youth mental health', *CYPN*, 29 September.

[37] Joe Lepper, 2023, 'Charity reveals "significant increase" in child destitution' *CYPN*, 23 August; Patrick Butler, 2023, 'More than 1 million UK children experienced destitution last year, study finds', *Guardian*, 24 October.

[38] Nadine Batchelor-Hunt, 2022, 'One on four young people forced to borrow money to buy food', yahoo!news, 3 November, https://news.yahoo.com/one-in-four-young-people-borrow-money-to-afford-food-cost-of-living-150105597.html.

concern for 16 per cent of the 500 11–24-year-olds surveyed.[39] A YMCA report also published that month—described by its Chief Executive Denise Hatton as 'grim reading'—showed that many young people living in supported accommodation were '... struggling to make ends meet', '... caught in a cycle of debt', and finding that '... when times were tough' food was the first to go. As a result, Hatton concluded, this already seriously 'disadvantaged' group were '... just existing, their aspirations halted' with many having 'increasingly retreated from everyday socialising'.[40] With particular implications for the provision of open youth work facilities, wider effects of the crisis on young people's everyday lives were identified by UK Youth in April 2023, with a third of those surveyed reporting that, to save money, they had had to cut back on their social life.[41]

One youth sector response to these financial pressures was the publication in early 2023 of a 'toolkit' by NYA designed to help youth workers provide sessions for young people on the cost-of-living crisis and money management.[42] Another was an inquiry into the crisis, and its effects on young people prompted by a UK Youth Parliament ballot in 2022 which had found that health and well-being was their highest priority issue. Launched in May 2023 by the British Youth Council's (BYC) youth select committee, the enquiry called in September for written submissions of evidence from the public, 'sector professionals' including those involved with charities and businesses, from 'marginalised communities' and from those on lower incomes.[43]

### In—and Out of—School

Evidence was also accumulating of how—often again, it seemed, in systemic ways—the schooling system was contributing to many of young people's 'failures'. Despite the Department of Employment saying it was

---

[39] Young Minds, 2022, 'Money and Mental Health', https://www.youngminds.org.uk/parent/parents-a-z-mental-health-guide/money-and-mental-health/.

[40] Denise Hatton, 2023, 'Young people need more help to prosper in 2023', *CYPN*, 3 January.

[41] Emily Harle, 2023, 'Young people fear cost-of-living crisis restricts employment opportunities', *CYPN*, 20 April.

[42] Emily Harle, 2023, 'Cost-of-living toolkit for youth workers launches', *CYPN*, 24 February.

[43] Emily Harle, 2023, 'Inquiry seeks views on how cost of living affects young people's wellbeing', *CYPN*, 18 August.

against the law, schools were making widespread use of student 'off-rolling', often in order to boost their exam results. According to research published in October 2019 by the Education Policy Institute (EPI), one in ten of a 61,000 national cohort of students who sat their GCSEs in 2017 had experienced a total of 69,000 'unexplained exits' at some point in their secondary school career.

The EPI report also provided significant insights into the operation of multi-academy trusts which—funded by the Department for Education (DfE) but independent of the local authority—were running more than one school across the country, with the larger ones running ten or more. One of neo-liberalism's most high-profile privatising initiatives, the trusts were 'showing above average rates overall' of school exclusions which included many students who were receiving free school meals and in care.[44] Two months later, FTT Education Datalab, an independent research body on education policy and practice, suggested that if all those 'off-rolled' students were factored into these kinds of calculations, even bigger learning gaps were likely to be revealed.[45]

Though also in 2019 the All Party Parliamentary Group (APPG) on knife crime—a top priority concern in this period—called for a review of why excluded children were not getting the full-time education they were legally entitled to,[46] by 2023 school suspensions had increased. One analysis of Department for Education (DfE) data published in September showed, for example, that these had risen post-pandemic by 30 per cent, with the number of children living in poverty who were affected up by 75 per cent. Here, too, significant racial inequalities were identified with Black Caribbean children 1.5 times more likely to be suspended than their white peers.[47]

More broadly, later EPI research[48] also revealed that between 2018 and 2019, for the first time since 2007, the gap within primary schools between

[44] Sally Weale, 2019, 'One in ten pupils removed from school rolls "to boost GCSE results"', *Guardian*, 11 October; Neil Puffett, 2019, 'One in ten children "removed from school unofficially", study finds', *CYPN*, 11 October.

[45] Joe Lepper, 2019, 'Off-rolling "hides true extent of pupil attainment gap" in schools', *CYPN*, 5 December.

[46] Neil Puffett, 2019, 'School exclusion "a tipping point" leading to knife crime, MPs warn', *CYPN*, 25 October.

[47] Emily Harle, 2023, 'Disadvantaged children worst hit by suspensions amid sharp rise', *CYPN*, 13 September.

[48] Sally Weale, 2020, 'Attainment gap between poor pupils and their peers in England is widening', *Guardian*, 26 August.

'disadvantaged' pupils and their wealthier classmates had also widened; and that by the time they took their General Certificate of Education (GCSE) examinations these pupils were still over 18 months behind their counterparts. In measuring attainment—'used in school to pinpoint what level a child should be achieving at their age'[49]—it found that the gap between Black Caribbean pupils and their white counterparts had also grown between 2011 and 2020, from 6.5 months to 10.9 months. By 2022, Covid had opened up these gaps further with, according to the grading systems used during the pandemic, 'disadvantaged' 16–19-year-olds 4.5 grades behind their more affluent peers.[50]

An Office of Qualifications and Examinations Regulation (Ofqual) report a year later also showed that since 2019, the gap between Black students and their white classmates in achieving an advanced-level grade or above had also increased;[51] while according to a Young Futures Foundation (YFF) survey published in October 2022, a quarter of its 2700 ethnic minority respondents thought their grades had suffered because of financial and mental health pressures.[52] Given these findings, it was perhaps unsurprising that by mid-2022, the EPI was concluding that, though the 'disadvantage gap' had 'come down over time', progress in narrowing the attainment gaps had been 'extremely slow'.[53]

Here, too, later developments—especially Covid and the cost-of-living crisis—had significant additional impacts. A Centre for Social Justice (CSJ) analysis of figures for autumn 2020, released in January 2022, revealed, for example, that nearly 100,000 young people had 'disappeared almost entirely from schools', with 'over 700 schools … missing an entire class-

[49] See https://www.google.com/search?q=attainment+gap+in+education&rlz=1C1N HXL_enGB772GB772&oq=Attaiment+gap+&gs_lcrp=EgZjaHJvbWU qCQgBEAAYDRiABDIGCAAQRRg5MgkIARAAGA0YgAQyCQgCEAAYDRi ABDIJCAMQABgNGIAEMgkIBBAAGA0YgAQyCQgFEAAYD RiABDIJCAYQABgNGIAEMgkIBxAAGA0YgAQyCQgIEAAYDRiABDIJCAkQA BgNGIAE0gEJMTU0ODFqMG03qAIAsIA&sourceid=chrome&ie=UTF-8.

[50] Amrit Virdi, 2023, 'Attainment gap for older pupils highest on record' report finds', *CYPN*, 18 December.

[51] Fiona Simpson, 2021, 'A-level results: attainment gap widens for disadvantaged pupils and Black students', *CYPN*, 10 August.

[52] Joe Lepper, 2022, 'Mental health and cost-of-living crisis "double threat" to young ethnic minority people', *CYPN*, 5 October.

[53] Nicole Weinstein, 2022. 'Questions over "extremely slow" progress to close attainment gap', *CYPN*, 18 July.

worth of children'.[54] By early 2023, these findings were being confirmed—for example:

- By an FTT Education Datalab enquiry that revealed a third of 15-year-olds had been 'persistently absent' from school since the previous September.[55]
- By government statistics showing that in the 2022 autumn term this was true of 25 per cent of pupils compared with 13.1 per cent in the same term in 2019.[56]
- By DfE attendance data which concluded that—with local councils finding that some children post-Covid were 'struggling to leave home'—absences in the spring term of 2023 were still 50 per cent higher than before the pandemic. This was resulting in 20 per cent of secondary school students missing 10 per cent or more of lessons and so being judged as 'persistently absent'.[57]

The effects of these absences were highlighted in October 2022 by research by the Covid Social Mobility and Opportunities Study (Cosmos), carried out in collaboration with the Sutton Trust and University College London. Four out of five of the young people questioned said their academic progress had suffered because of the pandemic, with state school pupils emerging as twice as likely as their peers in private schools to feel the deficits.[58] The 13,000 young people who contributed to another Sutton Trust survey published in early 2023 made some of these deficits explicit. Almost half, for example, said they hadn't caught up with learning missed because of Covid; almost 20 per cent, including those not infected, said that their GCSE grades were lower than they had expected; and 40 per

[54] Centre for Social Justice, 2022, *Lost but not forgotten: the reality of severe absence in schools post-lockdown*, January, https://www.centreforsocialjustice.org.uk/wp-content/uploads/2022/01/CSJ-Lost_but_not_forgotten-2.pdf.

[55] Richard Adams, 2023, 'Third of 15-year-olds persistently absent from school in England since September', *Guardian*, 10 February.

[56] Hazel Shearing, 2023, 'The number of pupils missing school in England has not returned to pre-Covid pandemic levels, according to official statistics', BBC News, 23 February, https://www.bbc.co.uk/news/education-64747813.

[57] Richard Adams and Carmen Aguilar Garcia, 2023, 'Rise in school absences since Covid driven by anxiety and lack of support, say English councils', *Guardian*, 24 April.

[58] Sally Weale, 2022, 'Four out of five pupils in England say progress suffered due to Covid', *Guardian*, 13 October.

cent said that that they'd been left unprepared for the next steps in education and training.[59]

Government initiatives intended to address these failings often turned out to be both inadequate in themselves and poorly implemented. Following its announcement in June 2020 of a £1 billion programme to help pupils catch up on their education—including £350 million for a National Tutoring Programme targeted at 'disadvantaged' children—it emerged that by the end of the year, only 150 of the promised 1000 'academic tutors' would actually be working in schools. Despite a further allocation of £700 million in February 2021 to fund these 'school catch-up plans', a month later the National Audit Office (NAO) was concluding that less than half of the 41,100 children who had started to receive the tuition were eligible for the 'disadvantaged' pupils' premium for improving educational outcomes in England. It also found that the ministers 'had no pre-existing plan for managing future mass disruption in schooling on the scale caused by Covid-19'.[60] Two months later, the government also rejected a House of Commons Education Select Committee proposal that post-pandemic catch-up support be focused on pupils' mental health needs.[61]

When in early 2023, the government announced that it was to withdraw its funding for helping 'disadvantaged' pupils to catch up on the learning lost because of Covid, schools were left to find money for this from existing budgets. This prompted the NAO to warn ministers that they needed to assess whether tutoring in schools would any longer be 'financially sustainable'.[62]

### *Finding—and Keeping—a Job*

Both before and during the Covid outbreak, closely interwoven with the struggles young people were having with their schooling, were increasing

---

[59] Amelia Hill, 2023, '"Debilitating" effects of the pandemic linger for Britain's young', *Guardian*, 30 January.

[60] Sally Weale, 2020, Only 150 of 1,000 mentors will be in England's schools before 2021', *Guardian*, 8 October; Joe Lepper, 2021, 'School catch-up schemes "not reaching" disadvantaged children, NAO warns', *CYPN*, 17 March.

[61] Joe Lepper, 2022, 'Government rejects call for Covid catch-up plan to focus on pupil mental health,' *CYPN*, 25 May.

[62] Joe Lepper, 2023, 'Catch-up tutoring's long-term future at risk, NAO warns', *CYPN*, 1 February.

uncertainties about whether they would get and then hold onto a job, particularly one that matched their aspirations and level of qualifications and offered some security and a promise of progression in the future.

Here, too, there is a significant backstory. A Resolution Foundation paper published in May 2020—that is, before the full impacts of the pandemic were being felt—focused on overlapping long-term issues left behind by previous recessions. It particularly highlighted that

> ... *for several years after having left education, employment rates across the cohorts that left education during the financial crisis (of 2008–10) were lower than for those who left education after it—with non-graduates experiencing the largest and longest scarring effects. Graduate 'recession leavers' experienced substantial hits too, but more in terms of being stuck in lower-skilled jobs than being out of work altogether. And for several years, both groups had lower hourly pay than their counterparts who left education after the recession.*[63]

The Resolution Foundation findings also highlighted wider embedded issues within the unemployed youth population. Some young people, for example, 'may have left education with an apprenticeship or a career destination in mind, only to find their sector of choice in severe contraction'; others, lacking basic numeracy and literacy skills, would have had 'few specific job destinations in their plans'. In January 2021, a DfE white paper sought to address these concerns by 'put(ting) an end to the illusion that a degree is the only route to success and a good job' and promising 'disadvantaged' young people better access to post-16 education and training generally.[64]

By then, however, the pandemic's constraining impacts on young people's job prospects were becoming increasingly clear. A report from the Office for National Statistics (ONS), for example, released in May 2020, estimated that 771,000 16–24-year-olds had been NEET in the first three months of the year—up by 6000 on a year before and by 8000 on the period October to December 2019.[65] Though the following year govern-

---

[63] Kathleen Henehan, 2020, *Class of 2020: Education leavers in the current crisis*, Resolution Foundation, May, p. 3, https://www.resolutionfoundation.org/app/uploads/2020/05/Class-of-2020.pdf.

[64] Joe Lepper, 2021, 'Careers guidance and training for disadvantaged groups among pledges to boost post-16 education', *CYPN*, 21 January.

[65] Nihara Krause, 2020, 'Transforming support for young people not in education, employment or training amid Covid-19', *CYPN*, 24 September.

ment data recorded the NEET figure as the lowest on record, by 2022, it had again increased significantly to 12.3 per cent of 16–24-year-olds.[66]

More broadly, ONS figures revealed that between August and October 2020, the number in that age group who were in employment fell by 90,000—the lowest on record.[67] Young people were also amongst those worst affected by the ending of the Treasury's furlough scheme in October 2020, with one in six 18–24-year-olds losing their jobs.[68] One conclusion of another Resolution Foundation enquiry report released nine months later was that this age group had been hardest hit by pandemic job losses, by the effects of furlough and by lost hours.[69]

Even though by the summer of 2021 that trend had started to reverse somewhat,[70] one in five 16–24-year-olds were still being recorded as long-term unemployed—that is, as out of work for more than a year[71]—while over 58 per cent of the jobs lost between February 2020 and January 2021 were those of under-25s.[72] Five years after taking their GCSEs, young people from poorer backgrounds were twice as likely as their peers still to be NEET;[73] the jobs they were finding were more likely to be in the gig economy and so less secure;[74] while 40 per cent of Black young people—three times the number of white workers of the same age—were without jobs.[75] Young women, too, were being disproportionately affected, accounting, for example, for almost all the increase in NEET

[66] GOV.UK, 2023, 'NEET aged 16–24': Headline figures – 2022', 2 March, https://explore-education-statistics.service.gov.uk/find-statistics/neet-statistics-annual-brief.

[67] Fiona Simpson, 2021, 'NEET young people "unable to cope with life" amid pandemic, Prince's Trust warns', *CYPN*, 19 January.

[68] Fiona Simpson, 2020, 'Young people" worst affected by post-furlough unemployment"', *CYPN*, 28 October.

[69] Neil Puffett, 2021, 'One in four young people worried mental health will impact work after pandemic' *CYPN*, 5 July.

[70] Fiona Simpson, 2021, 'Youth unemployment begins to fall as Covid-19 restrictions lift', *CYPN*, 17 August.

[71] Fiona Simpson, 2021, 'One in five young people facing long-term unemployment, ONS figures show', *CYPN* 15 June.

[72] Fiona Simpson, 2021, 'Under-25s hardest hit by Covid-19 job losses, ONS figures show', *CYPN*, 23 February.

[73] Fiona Simpson, 2022, Disadvantaged young people twice as likely to be NEET after GCSEs', *CYPN*, 24 August.

[74] Gwyn Topham, 2022, 'Young people who lost jobs in pandemic in UK "returning to insecure work"', *Guardian*, 31 January.

[75] Tobi Thomas, 2021, 'Black youth unemployment rate of 40% similar to time of Brixton riots, data shows', *Guardian*, 12 April.

numbers between June and September 2022.[76] By the end of 2022, two separate studies were also showing that 63 per cent of girls compared with 56 per cent of boys had changed their career plans.[77]

As these realities struck home, by then, almost a third of 5000 young people interviewed for one survey said that they didn't think they would ever be able to achieve their career ambitions.[78] Evidence from the YFF survey of 2700 ethnic minority young people referenced above had also already highlighted how, with a quarter struggling to pay for everyday items and services, one in ten had actually taken jobs with less opportunity for career progression.[79]

The wider context for all of this emerged from an Institute of Student Employers' report published in May 2020 which revealed that, as a result of Covid, 27 per cent of employers would be recruiting fewer graduates, 23 per cent fewer apprentices and 31 per cent fewer interns and placement students.[80] Though during 2021 the number overall of under-19s starting apprenticeships did begin to recover, this age group remained the only one whose apprentice numbers by early 2022 were below pre-pandemic levels—a situation which persisted into September.[81] By the end of the year, almost half of the young people who had signed up for an apprenticeship had given it up.[82]

By then, the Resolution Foundation was pointing to the lasting damage that unemployment could do to young people's careers and their broader living standards compared with their parents' generation.[83] Prince's Trust

[76] Joe Lepper, 2022, 'Surge in number of NEET young women', *CYPN*, 24 November.

[77] Joe Lepper, 2022, Study reveals pandemic's impact on young people's career and study plans', *CYPN*, 13 October; Joe Lepper, 2022, 'Disadvantaged young people "locked out of employment opportunities', *CYPN*, 8 December.

[78] Joe Lepper, 2022, Study reveals pandemic's impact on young people's career and study plans', *CYPN*, 13 October; Joe Lepper, 2022, 'Disadvantaged young people "locked out of employment opportunities', *CYPN*, 8 December.

[79] Joe Lepper, 2022, 'Mental health and cost-of-living crisis "double threat" to young ethnic minority people', *CYPN*, 5 October.

[80] Nihara Krause, 2020, 'Transforming the support for young people not in education, employment or training amid Covid-19', *CYPN*, 24 September.

[81] Joe Lepper, 2022, 'Apprentice numbers fall among young people post-pandemic', *CYPN*, 9 February; Fiona Simpson, 2022, 'Number of young people starting apprenticeships below pre-pandemic levels', *CYPN*, 8 September.

[82] *Guardian*, 2022, 'The *Guardian* view on apprenticeships: time to learn from past mistakes', 6 December.

[83] Richard Partington, 2020, Covid generation: UK youth unemployment "set to triple to 80's levels"', *Guardian*, 7 October.

research also warned that 40 per cent of NEET young people were feeling 'unable to cope with life'[84] so that, by early 2022, some of the biggest falls in young people's confidence and happiness were focused on employment prospects, training and qualifications.

Later Prince's Trust reports added to this evidence with the one published in February 2022 revealing that 22 per cent of those responding feared they would 'fail in life'.[85] Even when NEET levels overall began to fall below pre-pandemic levels,[86] for these young people the fearing 'fail-in-life' figure was 27 per cent, with 46 per cent saying that being unemployed 'made them feel hopeless'.[87] Unsurprisingly perhaps, the Trust's October report thus concluded that 60 per cent of 16–25-year-olds were anxious about their generation's future with one in three thinking that their job prospects would never recover.[88]

These findings were underpinned by those from a Youth Employment UK 'Youth Voice Census' released in September 2022 that, for example, only 14.2 per cent of young people were 'confident' they could find quality work in their area,[89] and by UK Youth research published six months later which found that 75 per cent of those responding continued to worry about its effects on their future job prospects.[90] One apparent practical consequence of these doubts was that, compared with 15 per cent of young people overall, a quarter of those from poorer backgrounds who had responded to the January 2023 Prince's Trust survey were planning to finish their education early so they could start earning money.[91] Another

[84] Fiona Simpson, 2021, 'NEET young people "unable to cope with life" amid pandemic, Prince's Trust warns', *CYPN*, 19 January.

[85] Prince's Trust/NatWest Group, 2022, *The Prince's Trust NatWest Youth Index 2022*, Princes Trust, February, https://www.princes-trust.org.uk/about-the-trust/news-views/princes-trust-natwest-youth-index-2022.

[86] Fiona Simpson, 2022, 'Proportion of NEET young people falls below pre-pandemic levels', *CYPN*, 3 March.

[87] Prince's Trust/NatWest Group, 2022.

[88] Amelia Hill, 2022, 'Covid has left a third of young people feeling life is out of control – study', *Guardian*, 3 October.

[89] Youth Employment UK, 2022, *Youth Voice Census: 2022 Report*, 6 September, https://www.youthemployment.org.uk/dev/wp-content/themes/yeuk/files/youth-voice-census-report-2022.pdf.

[90] Emily Harle, 2023, 'Young people fear cost-of-living crisis restricts employment opportunities', *CYPN*, 20 April.

[91] Amelia Hill, 2023, '"Debilitating" effects of the pandemic linger for Britain's young', *Guardian*, 30 January.

consequence, identified by a Social Mobility Foundation survey carried out in 2023, was that some 85 per cent of 2000 16–18-year-olds felt they would need to move from where they lived to get better job opportunities. Significant regional differences emerged here with high figures recorded particularly for the east of England, the north-west and Yorkshire.[92]

By mid-2023, effects of the cost-of-living crisis on job expectations and possibilities were also being documented. A third of the young people polled by the LadBible Group, for example, said that the crisis was interlinked with a lack of self-confidence and work experience and that mental health problems were also significant contributory factors. As a result, 57 per cent said that in the previous two years, they had lowered their career aspirations.[93]

These growing concerns prompted some (albeit limited and sometimes controversial) policy and practice responses. In September 2020, an APPG inquiry into Covid's economic impact on young people was announced,[94] and a £2 billion Kickstart scheme was launched which by April 2022 had approved 305,000 job placements and found jobs for 162,000 young people.[95] As an example of a more grounded—and more modest—initiative, in January 2021, the social enterprise Catch 22, supported by the investment bank JP Morgan Chase, set up a programme to help into work some 400 young people who were facing what were called 'employment barriers'.[96]

Two months later, however, the NYA was still pointing to a need for higher government investment to guarantee young people the help they

[92] Sammy Gecsoyler, 'Young people in England feel they must move for better opportunities', *Guardian*, 15 September.

[93] Andy Hillier, 2023, 'Young people ditching ambitions over UK cost of living crisis, research finds', *Guardian*, 19 September; Amrit Virdi, 2023, 'Lack of opportunity and low confidence key barriers to entering work, young people say' *CYPN*, 20 September.

[94] Fiona Simpson, 2020, 'MPs launch inquiry into economic impact of Covid-19 on young people', *CYPN*, 8 September.

[95] GOV.UK, 2022, '7 in 10 young people in work 4 months after leaving government's Kickstart Scheme', 14 July, https://www.google.com/search?rlz=1C1NHXL_enGB772 GB772&cs=0&q=How+successful+is+the+Kickstart+scheme%3F&sa=X&ved=2ahUKEwjd usbssMH6AhVEoVwKHZswAv8Qzmd6BAgIEAU&biw=1600&bih=757&dpr=1.

[96] Neil Puffett, 2021, '#Chance4children: Employment programme launches to help young people into work', *CYPN*, 18 January.

needed to find jobs and get training. These, it argued, were initiatives which should involve 'trained youth workers (to) provide long term relationships that young people value, and ensure there is cliff-edge support when (they) reach 18 …'.[97]

## Finding Somewhere to Live

Even before the pandemic, independent, affordable and secure housing had become out of reach for many young people. In 2019, for example, ONS research revealed that over the previous two decades, the number of 20–24-year-olds who had returned to live with their parents had risen by 46 per cent—from 2.4 million to 3.5 million.[98] Compared to ten years before, by the time the 2021 census was carried out, this was true for 15 per cent (700,000) more 'non-dependent children' in England and Wales (average age 24).[99]

Reflecting similar shifts, a Resolution Foundation survey published in December 2021 concluded that, since the 1980s, home ownership amongst the 25–34-year-old age group had fallen by almost a half—from 51 per cent to 28 per cent. Though their preference was to buy rather than rent, 80 per cent of respondents said they didn't have earnings to do that.[100] By January 2022, only 66 per cent of 25-year-olds and under expected to ever be able to buy—a proportion which fell to 37 per cent among those who were NEET.[101]

Lurking increasingly within these worries—especially as Covid and its restrictions impacted—was the threat of homelessness. According to a Centrepoint/Co-operative Bank survey published in October 2020, almost a quarter of 16–24-year-olds were concerned that, if they lost their

[97] Joe Lepper, 2021,' NYA: "Fundamental change" needed to tackle unemployment crisis', *CYPN*, 24 March.

[98] Patrick Collinson, 2019, 'Record numbers of young adults in UK living with parents', *Guardian*, 15 November.

[99] Robert Booth and Michael Goodier, 2023, 'Number of adults living with parents in England and Wales rises by 700,000 in a decade', *Guardian*, 10 May.

[100] Helen Crane, 2021, 'Home ownership among young people has nearly HALVED since the 1980s, report says', *This is Money*, 3 December, https://www.thisismoney.co.uk/money/mortgageshome/article-10267295/Home-ownership-young-people-nearly-HALVED-1980s.html.

[101] Kate Ng, 2022, 'A quarter of young people don't think they will ever feel financial secure', *Independent*, 6 January.

income, this would happen to them.[102] The report coincided with the release of data showing that the number of 16–25-year-olds who were actually sleeping rough in London had risen to record levels—up by 47 per cent, from 250 a year earlier to 368; the number of young women sleeping rough had doubled; and that there was disproportionately high number identifying as LGBTQ+.[103]

Other data from January 2022 indicated that since the first lockdown in March 2020, 11 per cent of rough sleepers had been under 25, and calls to Centrepoint's homelessness helpline were a quarter up on pre-pandemic levels.[104] By the beginning of 2023, the number of young people contacting their local authority for help with housing had also risen—by 8 per cent—though for the 12 months to the previous April, only two-thirds who did this were actually assessed. This, according to Centrepoint, meant that some 40,000 may have been denied a check on their eligibility.[105] Its follow-up study for the financial year 2021–22, published in late 2023, revealed that these numbers had risen further, with one in every 52 (119,300) of the 16–24-year-olds surveyed facing homelessness and only 68 per cent of the 112,500 who had sought help actually being assessed by their local council.[106]

By then, the chances of some 85,000 young people finding somewhere affordable to live were judged to have been even further reduced by the late-2020 government decision to abandon plans to build 200,000 new 'starter homes' to be sold at 20 per cent discount—a move described by the House of Commons Public Accounts Committee as 'deplorable'.[107] This situation was exacerbated further in January 2023 by government's

---

[102] *Charity Today*, 2020, 'Fear of homelessness spike amongst young people', 8 October, https://www.charitytoday.co.uk/fear-of-homelessness-spike-amongst-young-people/.

[103] Sarah Marsh, 2020, 'Covid restrictions push more under-25s than ever to sleep rough in London, charities say', *Guardian*, 31 October; Fiona Simpson, 2022, 'Youth organisations rally to support young rough sleepers', *CYPN*, 20 January.

[104] Fiona Simpson, 2022, 'Youth organisations rally to support rough sleepers', *CYPN*, 20 January; Fiona Simpson, 2021, 'Youth homelessness up by a quarter on pre-pandemic levels, Centrepoint reveals' 15 December.

[105] Joe Lepper, 2023, 'Youth homelessness numbers rocket amid cost-of-living crisis', *CYPN*, 22 February 23.

[106] Fiona Simpson, 2023, 'Record number of young people seeking homelessness support', *CYPN*, 6 November.

[107] Richard Booth, 2020, 'Government scrapping affordable starter homes "deplorable", say MPs', *Guardian*, 9 December.

announcement that the mandatory target of 300,000 new homes a year was to be dropped, prompting nearly 40 local authorities to pause or scale back their house-building plans.[108]

## MENTAL HEALTH IMPACTS

These accumulating pressures on young people's everyday lives had impacts which, despite their underlying structural roots, could by many be experienced as personal 'failure', with often serious consequences for what came increasingly to be labelled their 'emotional wellbeing'. Not all the evidence was negative—a Youth Sport Trust report of a survey of nearly 5500 13–15-year-olds, for example, published in November 2023, revealed that participation in sport could be significant in predicting their self-belief and mental toughness.[109] And though a range of research was indicating that social media and the internet more broadly were, sometimes seriously, exacerbating these anxieties,[110] debates also continued on how widespread and how lasting these effects were.[111]

While acknowledging a range of government responses, in her January 2023 article (quoted above), YMCA Chief Executive Denise Hatton highlighted a 'significant challenge' particularly relevant to youth workers—that

*… (as) social and leisure opportunities become a distant memory … isolation and detachment is having a significant impact on the confidence of some young people … with ever growing implications for their mental health ….[112]*

---

[108] Kiran Stacey and Jessica Elgot, 2023, 'New homes at risk as English authorities cut housebuilding plans', *Guardian*, 15 January.

[109] Fiona Simpson, 2023, 'Sports participation boosts wellbeing in young teenagers, research funds', *CYPN*, 30 November.

[110] See, for example, Young Minds, 2022, 'A third of young people feel trapped on social media', 5 December, https://www.youngminds.org.uk/about-us/media-centre/press-releases/a-third-of-young-people-feel-trapped-on-social-media/; NIHR, 2023, 'The impact of social media use on young people's mental health', 5 April, https://sphr.nihr.ac.uk/news-and-events/news/the-impact-of-social-media-use-on-young-peoples-mental-health/#:~:text=While%20some%20studies%20have%20linked,strengthen%20bonds%2C%20and%20reduce%20loneliness; Hannah Devlin, 2024, 'Revealed: almost half of British teens feel addicted to social media, study says', *Guardian*, 2 January.

[111] Gaby Hinsliff, 2024, 'Not Going Out', *Guardian Saturday,*10 Feb. 24.

[112] Denise Hatton, 2023, 'Young people need more help to prosper in 2023', *CYPN*, 3 January.

Here, as essential balancing context, it is important to note one of the conclusions drawn by Lucy Foulkes in her paper also referenced above: that 84 per cent of the 5–16-year-olds surveyed *'didn't* meet the criteria for a (mental health) disorder' (emphasis in the original). She still, however, started from the proposition that 'if you're ever going to experience mental illness, it will most likely start in your adolescent years'.[113]

### *The Pre-Covid Evidence …*

In December 2019, an Office for Economic Co-operation and Development (OECD) report on education provision in its 38 member countries concluded that 'schoolchildren in Britain are more likely to be miserable and less likely to think their lives have meaning compared with children in other countries'. It also found that 15-year-olds in the UK had experienced 'the biggest declines in life satisfaction since … 2015, with barely half reporting that they were satisfied with their lives'.[114]

Similar findings emerged from the Millennium Cohort Study tracking the lives of 19,000 'nationally representative' children and young people born in the UK between 2000 and 2002. According to its September 2017 report, 'at the age of 14, when children self-reported their own symptoms, 24% of girls and 9% of boys were suffering from high symptoms of depression'.[115] By the time its 2021 report appeared, it was concluding that, by the age of 17, 7 per cent of the cohort had attempted suicide with almost one in four saying that they had self-harmed in the previous year.[116] Though published well before it could assess the full Covid-19 impacts, it also warned that fallout from the pandemic would probably make matters worse.

Findings by the Children's Commissioner in England released a month earlier—that, for example, compared with three years before, children's 'clinically significant mental health conditions' had risen by 50 per cent by

[113] Lucy Foulkes, 2021, 'Covid's "lost generation" may be more resilient than we think', *Guardian*, 2 June.

[114] Richard Adams and Caelainn Barr, 2019, 'Many UK children feel their lives have no meaning, survey finds', *Guardian*, 4 December.

[115] Institute of Education, 2017, *Mental ill-health among children of the new century*, UCL, September.

[116] Sarah Marsh, 2021, 'About 7% of UK children have attempted suicide by age of 17 – study', *Guardian*, 22 February.

July 2020—added to this evidence.[117] Referencing sources such as the Children's Society and United Nations International Children's Emergency Fund (UNICEF), by October of that year, the DfE was thus having to acknowledge that 'the wellbeing of children in England and the UK remains low compared with other countries ...'.[118]

### ... And the Covid Fallout

The 2021 Millennium Cohort Study's prediction of Covid's ongoing mental health effects proved to be only too accurate.

- Just three months into the pandemic, in May 2020, 32 per cent of over a thousand 16–25-year-olds responding to that year's Prince's Trust survey said they felt 'overwhelmed' by feelings of panic and anxiety and 69 per cent that their life was 'on hold'.[119]
- A paper published jointly by the NYA and Brook, the young people's sexual health and wellbeing charity, found that 72 per cent of the young people contacted reported a decline in their mental health during lockdown.[120]
- A year later, the Royal College of Psychiatrists talked of England having been pushed into 'the grip of a mental health crisis' as in the previous year record, numbers had sought help for problems such as anxiety, depression and eating disorders. Between April and December 2020, it was reported, there had been 28 per cent more referrals of under-18s than in the same period in 2019.[121]

[117]Joe Lepper, 2021, 'Serious mental health conditions in children up by 50 per cent in three years', *CYPN*, 28 January.

[118]Department of Education, 2020, *State of the nation 2020: children and young people's wellbeing*, GOV.UK, 10 October, https://www.gov.uk/government/publications/state-of-the-nation-2020-children-and-young-peoples-wellbeing.

[119]Fiona Simpson, 2020, 'Young people "overwhelmed by panic and anxiety" during lockdown' *CYPN*, 21 May.

[120]Fiona Simpson, 2020, 'Concerns over "huge decline" in young people's mental health during lockdown', *CYPN*, 19 August.

[121]Denis Campbell, 2021, 'Extent of mental health crisis in England at "terrifying" level', *Guardian*, 9 April.

- By May 2022, the NHS's own figures were showing that since February 2020, the 'open referral' of 'troubled' children and young people in England had risen by 54 per cent.[122]
- By the following September ONS, data analysed by the youth mental health charity YoungMinds was indicating that 198 15–19-year-olds had taken their own lives in 2021—the highest in 30 years and up by a third from the 147 recorded in 2020.[123] Nine months later, its analysis of NHS Digital data revealed that in 2022, a record 1.4 million children and young people had sought NHS help with mental health problems. Over 800,000 under-18-year-olds had been referred to Child and Adolescent Mental Health Services (CAMHS) for treatment for anxiety, depression, eating disorders and other psychological problems, with 58 per cent of young people saying that the most common cause of damage to their mental health were money worries.[124]
- According to the February 2022 Prince's Trust Youth Index survey, '… scores for almost all areas attributed to wellbeing … (were) at their lowest to date'. These particularly revealed a 'notable decrease in happiness' about relationships with friends and family and in confidence.[125]
- A monthly survey of 51,000 adults carried out by King's College, London, between April 2020 and December 2022, published in July 2023, revealed a sharp increase in 'distress' among young adults. In 12 months up to December 2023—by which time the cost-of-living crisis was also having its effects—this rose from 13.6 per cent of those responding to 20.2 per cent.[126]

[122] Denis Campbell, 2022, 'Record 420,000 children and month in England treated for mental health problems', *Guardian*, 23 May.

[123] Nicole Weinstein, 2022, 'Campaigners warn of "alarming" rise in teenage suicides', *CYPN*, 14 September.

[124] Denis Campbell, 2023, 'Record number of children seek mental health help from NHS England', *Guardian*, 27 June.

[125] Prince's Trust/NatWest Group, 2022, *The Prince's Trust NatWest Youth Index 2022*, Prince's Trust, February, https://www.princes-trust.org.uk/about-the-trust/news-views/princes-trust-natwest-youth-index-2022.

[126] Ian Sample, 2023, 'Distress in England's young adults has risen sharply since Covid, study shows', *Guardian*, 6 July.

32

The Prince's Trust research quoted above also identified often significant mental health differences in relation to class, ethnicity and gender:

- As well as indicating lower GCSE or Scottish Standards examination grade results overall, pupils on free school meals—the Index's measure of low income—recorded a six-point drop in their overall 'confidence and happiness' score compared with those from more affluent backgrounds.
- Also on the 'confidence and happiness' measure, young people from minority ethnic backgrounds scored three points lower than their white counterparts.
- Compared with 19 per cent of young men, 26 per cent of young women felt they would never recover from the pandemic's emotional effects and a quarter that they were going to fail in life.

Other studies confirmed these gender differences—including in relation to gender identity.

- One released by Girlguiding in September 2021 found that the proportion of 7–21-year-old girls and young women who said they felt 'unhappy most of the time' had risen in the previous three years from 17 to 32 per cent, with increased loneliness being reported by 77 per cent of those identifying as LGBQ.[127] By September 2023, Girlguiding polling was indicating that girls' and young women's happiness was at its lowest level since 2009 with 9 out of 10 7- to 21-year-olds saying they were worried or anxious and only 17 per cent that they felt very happy.[128]
- Compared with just 7 per cent of boys, 22 per cent of the girls who responded to an autumn 2022 survey of 40,000 young people in Manchester carried out by the BeeWell project said they were experiencing 'serious emotional difficulties'.[129]

[127] Derren Hayes, 2021, 'Pandemic and online pressures drive decline in girls' happiness', *CYPN*, 8 September.

[128] Robert Booth, 2023, 'The sharpest drop in happiness has been among seven to 10 year olds', *Guardian*, 13 September.

[129] Branwen Jeffreys, 2022, 'Girls face more pressure to be a perfect teenager', BBC News, March https://www.bbc.co.uk/news/education-60771915.

- Cosmos findings released in November added to the evidence that such problems were particularly common amongst girls.[130]

## Wider Impacts

The mental health effects of the day-to-day pressures facing young people, examined earlier in this chapter, also came to demand growing attention. As well as raising concerns about low levels of pupils' post-lockdown return to school,[131] a study by the National Centre for Social Research (NatCen), published in July 2021, found that children experiencing poor mental health were three times less likely than their peers to pass five GCSEs.[132] A year later, a report from the Learning and Work Institute and The Prince's Trust concluded that 'key barriers' for those who were unemployed and wanting a job included mental health issues such as low self-esteem.[133] By early 2023, the Association of School and College Leaders was also suggesting that many pupil absences were the result of their high levels of stress and anxiety and long waits for mental health treatment.[134]

Once it took hold, for under-25-year-olds, the cost-of-living crisis also began to have 'considerable impact' on their mental health.[135] By the autumn of 2022, for example, The Prince's Trust survey was revealing that 60 per cent of 16–25-year-olds were saying that, having lived through a pandemic, they were now scared for their generation's future,[136] while a

---

[130] Joe Lepper, 2023, 'Almost half of young people "have mental health problems post-pandemic', *CYPN*, 22 November.

[131] Fiona Simpson, 2020, 'Children raise concerns about impact of school return on mental health', *CYPN*, 27 August.

[132] Helen Pidd, 2021, 'Poor mental health leaves pupils three times less likely to pass five GCSE's', *Guardian*, 26 July.

[133] Fiona Simpson, 2022, 'Mental health problems prevent NEET young people from finding work, study shows', *CYPN* 19 July.

[134] Hazel Shearing, 2023, 'The number of pupils missing school in England has not returned to pre-Covid pandemic levels, according to official statistics', BBC News, 23 February, https://www.bbc.co.uk/news/education-64747813.

[135] Fiona Simpson, 2022, 'Cost-of-living crisis has "significant" impact on youth mental health', *CYPN*, 29 September.

[136] Amelia Hill, 2022, 'Covid has left a third of young people feeling life is cout of contol – study', *Guardian*, 3 October.

report commissioned by the YFF warned that 'the negative impacts of the cost-of-living crisis are more pronounced among non-white groups ...'.[137]

## *And in Response ...?*

As these pressures built, it became increasingly clear that, despite small-scale initiatives from outside the NHS such as the Co-op Foundation's 'Lonely Not Alone' campaign aimed at 10–25-year-olds,[138] the services available to young people for dealing with their mental health struggles were—to say the least—limited.

Reporting in November 2019, for example, Young Minds found that, even pre-Covid, 75 per cent of General Practitioners (GPs) were questioning whether their under-18 referrals to CAMHS would get treated.[139] With overall numbers referred with mental health problems doubling in just three months to 200,000, evidence released in September 2021 suggested that 'even under-18s with an eating disorder or psychosis were being refused care by over stretched NHS Child and Adolescent Mental Health Services'.[140] By April 2022, a survey of over 1000 young people was concluding that by then, CAMHS teams were even more overloaded because of the pandemic's impacts on this age group.[141]

These pressures were further illustrated by data which emerged in early 2023—that, for example, in the previous year, 73 per cent of acute hospital trusts in England had recorded under-18-year-olds spending over 650,000 hours waiting in Accident and Emergency (A&E) departments for responses to their mental health concerns.[142]

Meanwhile, the issue absorbing the Cabinet and many Conservative MPs more widely at this time was not how to fill the gaps in these services

---

[137] Joe Lepper, 2022, 'Mental Health and cost-of-living crisis "double threat" to young ethnic minority people', *CYPN*, 5 October.

[138] Joe Lepper, 2021, 'Online campaign launches to tackle youth loneliness', *CYPN*, 14 October.

[139] Denis Campbell, 2019, 'Under-18s being denied urgent mental health treatment, say GPs', *Guardian*, 7 November.

[140] Andrew Gregory, 2021, 'Children's NHS mental health referrals double in pandemic' *Guardian*, 23 Sept; Denis Campbell, 2022, 'Swamped NHS mental health services turning away children, say GPs', *Guardian*, 3 April.

[141] Denis Campbell, 2022, 'Swamped mental health services turning away children, say GPs', *Guardian*, 4 April.

[142] Denis Campbell, 2023, Children in mental health crisis spent more than 900,000 hours in A&E in England, *Guardian*, 9 February.

but how to reduce the size of the state and further liberate 'the market'.[143] This prompted Chancellor Jeremy Hunt to bring forward the date of the 2024 Budget to March so that, ahead of the general election, he could further cut public spending and lower taxes—moves which the IFS predicted would result in a period of austerity 'more painful still' than the one following the 2008 financial crash.[144]

[143] See, for example, Aubrey Allegretti, 2023, 'Sunak's Commons majority in danger as 60 Tories join Truss group urging tax cuts', *Guardian*, 3 October 2023.
[144] Richard Partington, Kiran Stacey and Phillip Inman, 2023, 'Hunt's tax cuts mean austerity "more painful" that under Osborne, warns IFS', *Guardian*, 23 November.

# CHAPTER 3

# Funding Youth Work

**Abstract** Though some local open youth work facilities were reinstalled, throughout the period covered by this book, they also continued to face cuts. Avoiding any explicit commitment to their full reinstatement, the government created a range of 'gesture' Funds, many with specific targets on, for example, supporting uniformed organisations, youth unemployment, Covid-19 support, violence and antisocial behaviour and 'at risk' young people. Though having a broader reach, the Youth Investment Fund (YIF) provides a revealing case study of the government's funding strategy which, to help fill some of the continuing gaps, left open youth work reliant still on contributions from charities and the business world.

**Keywords** Budget cuts • Targeting • 'Gesture' funding • Youth Investment Fund (YIF) • Charities • Business world

## THE 'AUSTERITY DECADE'—AND BEYOND

Underpinned, still, by the neo-liberal priorities outlined in Chap. 1, throughout this period, the financial impacts of a decade of austerity severely constrained state-funded open youth work and its capacity to respond to the growing pressures young people were having to negotiate.

The local authority context was highlighted by the Local Government Association's (LGA) warning in October 2018 that, with councils having already lost 60p in the pound of their government funding since 2010, the Treasury's Revenue Support Grant for council services was due to be cut in 2019–20 by a further £1.3 billion or 36 per cent.[1] By late 2023/early 2024, even though English councils had by then in total sold public assets worth some £15 billion, including youth clubs and community centres,[2] some were declaring themselves bankrupt. They included Nottingham which, with a budget gap of £50 million, announced the closure in December 2023 of an adventure playground and 'a play and youth centre'; and Birmingham, the largest local authority in Europe, whose planned budget cuts for 2024–25 threatened the majority of its 18 youth centres and projects.[3]

In a report released in early 2023, the YMCA acknowledged that in the previous financial year, half of local authorities had managed a 'hugely helpful' increase in spending on holiday activities and food support.[4] One example was the London borough of Tower Hamlets which in July that year announced a new £13.7 million Youth Service budget to fund a 'youth space' and free summer holiday activities in every ward in the borough.[5] However, the YMCA report judged many of these responses '… not a fitting replacement for year-round youth services'.

Given the ongoing cuts in the government's financial support for local authorities, it was hardly surprising that their spending specifically on youth services continued to fall—in 2017–18 alone, for example, by £32 million compared to the previous year.[6] In England and Wales, over the whole of this period councils' Youth Service budgets were cut by £1 billion, with their spending per young person falling from an average of

[1] LGA, 2018, 'Local services face further £1.3 billion government funding cut in 2019/20', LGA, 1 October, https://www.local.gov.uk/about/news/local-services-face-further-ps13-billion-government-funding-cut-201920.

[2] Robyn Vinter, 2023, '£15bn of public assets sold by English councils since 2010 amid budget shortfalls', *Guardian*, 21 September.

[3] Richard Partington, 2023, 'As Britain's town hall services crumble, the case for reform is overwhelming', *Guardian*, 2 October; Jessica Murray, 2023, 'Nottingham city council plans cuts to libraries, care homes and youth services', *Guardian*, 12 December; Ben Godfrey, 2024, 'Fears for city's youth as clubs face budget cuts', BBC Midlands today, 11 March, https://www.bbc.co.uk/news/articles/cndjyke0lz0o.

[4] Joe Lepper, 2023, 'Wales spending twice as much as England on youth services, YMCA finds', *CYPN*, 1 March.

[5] Joe Lepper, 2023, 'London council launches £13.7m youth offer', *CYPN*, 19 July.

[6] Joanne Parkes, 2019, '"Spending on children's centres and youth services down by £140m"', *CYPN*, 9 January.

£136 to £54. Across the country, this resulted by 2017–18 in the closure of 760 youth centres, the loss of 4500 youth work posts and 139,000 youth service places and at least 35,000 fewer hours of 'outreach work'.[7] That year student numbers on approved youth and community work courses also fell—from 1300 in 2009–10 to 432[8] (see Chap. 8).

The Covid-19 lockdowns later added to these impacts, with Girlguiding, for example, announcing that, following the forced cancellation of many of its regular residential 'adventure' programmes, it was closing five of its activity centres.[9] This happened even though by then a £19 million DCMS Million Hours Fund was providing bursaries to access 'adventures away from home' for some 7500 young people from 'disadvantaged backgrounds across England' living in areas with high rates of anti-social behaviour.[10]

In a Barnardo's briefing paper focused on young people's increased risk of being coerced into criminal or sexual activity, one young person very vividly captured the more personal impacts of the lost youth work facilities:

> *Youth Clubs. That's what we need. Youth club used to be sick and then one day they just disappeared. There was bare youth clubs … they just want the kids on the streets now. They don't have nothing.*[11]

Harder evidence of the positive 'wider societal benefits' of government investment in these facilities had also by then emerged from research

[7] Unison, 2014, *The Damage: UK youth services*, Unison, August; Unison, 2016, *The Damage: A Future at Risk – cuts to youth services*, August, Unison; Hannah Richardson (2016), 'Youth services heading towards collapse, says union', BBC News, 12 August, https://www.bbc.co.uk/news/education-37046967.

[8] Rob Merrick, 2021, 'Hundreds of millions of pounds promised government cash for "collapsing" youth services shelved', *Independent*, 31 January; Unison, 2019, *Youth services at breaking point*, April, https://www.unison.org.uk/content/uploads/2019/04/Youth-services-report-04-2019.pdf; Derren Hayes', 2017, 'Youth work student numbers plunge by 28 per cent', *CYPN*, 4 May.

[9] Emily Harle, 2023, 'Youth organisations face changing landscape of residential schemes', *CYPN*, 30 August.

[10] Fiona Simpson, 'Sector hopes updated sufficiency rules will boost access to youth services', *CYPN*, 24 October; NYA Email 2023, 'Other sector investments announced this week', NYA Network, 29 September; GOV.UK, 2023, 'Lucy Frazer's speech at the Connected Futures conference', 12 October 2023, https://www.gov.uk/government/speeches/lucy-frazers-speech-at-the-connected-futures-conference.

[11] Fiona Simpson, 2023, 'Youth work investment "key" to reducing exploitation over school holidays, Barnardo's says', *CYPN*, 2 June.

commissioned by UK Youth, published in November 2022.[12] This, for example, concluded that the direct economic value of youth work was then £5.7b billion' and its indirect economic value at least £3.2 billion. The latter, it suggested, was made up of savings of £1.7 billion from improved health (including mental health) outcomes, £0.8 billion from increased youth employment and education, and £0.5 billion from reduced spending on criminal justice costs and 'anti-social behaviour'. These findings were complemented by NYA research published in November 2023 which concluded that in the London boroughs worst affected by the youth centre closures 10- to 15-year-olds' participation in crime after 2010 had increased by 10 per cent.[13]

Over the decade, the government created a range of new Funds targeted at 'youth issues' such as 'violent crime', 'hotspots', 'youth loneliness', 'youth unemployment' and 'arts and sports'. In addition to the Million Hours Fund previously referenced—and with at least one failing to deliver[14]—their titles included 'Youth Engagement',[15] 'Early Intervention',[16] 'Uniformed Youth',[17] 'Building Connections',[18] 'Integrated Communities Innovation',[19] 'Youth Accelerator',[20] 'Youth

[12] UK Youth, 2022, *Economic Value of Youth Work: Summary*, Frontier Economics/UK Youth, November; Fiona Simpson, 2022, 'Youth work investment could save public services £3,2BN per year', *CYPN*, 11 November.

[13] Amrit Virdi, 2023, 'Youth centre closures linked to increased risk of youth crime, NYA warns', *CYPN*, 6 November.

[14] Fiona Simpson, 2021, 'DCMS fails to spend £17m Youth Covid Support Fund, NAO investigation finds,' *CYPN*, 23 March.

[15] GOV.UK, 2014, 'Youth Engagement Fund: prospectus', 23 May, updated 3 October, https://www.gov.uk/government/publications/youth-engagement-fund-prospectus; James Ronicle and Kate Smith, 2020, *Youth Engagement Fund: Final* Report, Ecorys UK, March, https://assets.publishing.service.gov.uk/government/uploads/system/uploads/attachment_data/file/886650/YEF_Evaluation_Report_.pdf.

[16] Joe Lepper, 2018, 'Call to boost after-school youth work to reduce risk of violence', *CYPN*, 11 October; October; Gabriella Jozwiak, 2018, 'Home Office announces £18m for youth projects to tackle serious violence', *CYPN*, 12 November.

[17] Joe Lepper, 2019, 'Deprived areas to get 6,000 new youth group places', *CYPN*, 8 January.

[18] Joanne Parkes, 2019, 'Youth fund for transforming spaces awards £1.5m', *CYPN*, 17 January.

[19] Nina Jacobs, 2019, 'Community integration fund benefits youth projects' *CYPN*, 22 May.

[20] Joanne Parkes, 2019, 'Government announces £12m boost for youth sector', *CYPN*, 25 October; Fiona Simpson, 2020, 'Youth projects to benefit from £7m boost', *CYPN*, 30 January; Nina Jacobs, 2020, 'Youth groups benefit from £1.16m funding', *CYPN*, 6 March.

Endowment',[21] 'Youth Covid-19 Support',[22] 'Connected Futures',[23] 'Youth Investment'[24] and (allocated £1.5 million by the DCMS to help implement the government's 'levelling-up agenda' in 'underserved' areas) 'Uniformed Youth New Groups'.[25]

In March 2023, it also announced that some of the £892 million of 'dormant assets' were to be used to establish 'outdoor learning schemes' in England. This received immediate support from an 'Access Unlimited' coalition whose members included the Scouts and Girlguiding.[26] It was far from clear, however, how much of the money was for open youth work as six months later DCMS Minister Lucy Frazer explained that £15 million of the assets were for a 'Building Futures programme' focused on giving 5000 14- to 16-year-olds 'mentoring and wrap around support'.[27]

Even when taken together, however, these funding commitments still fell far short of that YMCA call for a 'fitting replacement for year-round youth services'[28]—particularly those providing open youth work. This was illustrated by the findings of the NYA's National Youth Sector Census published in September 2023—for example, at a time when a fifth of youth work providers had three- to six-month waiting lists, a quarter of

[21] Fiona Simpson, 2020, 'Youth Endowment Fund announces 130 organisations granted share of £6.5m', *CYPN*. 22July; Joe Lepper, 2020, 'Youth Endowment Fund launches 10-year strategy to tackle youth violence' *CYPN*, 7 October; *Children and Young People Now*, 2020, 'Youth Endowment Fund', *CYPN*, 27 October.

[22] GOV.UK, 2020, 'Government announces £16.5 million youth covid-19 support fund', 25 November, https://www.gov.uk/government/news/government-announces-165-million-youth-covid-19-support-fund; Fiona Simpson, 2020, 'Spending Review: What has Rishi Sunak pledged for children and young people?', *CYPN*, 25 November.

[23] Fiona Simpson, 2022, 'Seven areas with high youth unemployment to benefit from £16m fund', *CYPN*, 21 July.

[24] Joanne Parkes, 2019A, '"Javid announces £500m for youth fund"' *CYPN*, 30 September.

[25] GOV.UK, 2022, 'Uniformed Youth New Groups Fund Grant Competition Guidance', updated 21 September, https://www.gov.uk/government/publications/uniformed-youth-new-groups-fund-grant-competition/uniformed-youth-new-groups-fund-grant-competition-guidance; Joe Lepper, 2022, 'Uniformed youth groups offered £1.5m to expand into disadvantaged areas', *CYPN*, 8 September.

[26] Emily Harle, 2023, 'Outdoor learning schemes to benefit from £892m fund', *CYPN*, 24 March.

[27] GOV.UK, 2023, 'Lucy Frazer's speech at the Connected Futures conference', 12 October, https://www.gov.uk/government/speeches/lucy-frazers-speech-at-the-connected-futures-conference.

[28] Joe Lepper, 2023, 'Wales spending twice as much as England on youth services, YMCA finds', *CYPN*, 1 March.

voluntary sector organisations had less than six months' reserves.[29] According to NYA's Director of Youth Work, by mid-2023, these financial pressures were being exacerbated by the cost-of-living crisis.[30] However, when the LGA called for a commitment in that month's Treasury Autumn Statement for additional funding for youth work, Frazer dismissed this on the grounds that some of the £60 million budget already allocated to local authorities was for fulfilling their statutory duty to provide youth services.[31]

### The Youth Investment Fund: A Case Study of 'Gesture' Funding

The Youth Investment Fund (YIF) attracted particular attention within the youth work sector, not least because for open youth work it both promised much and revealed the limits and unreliability of these forms of government funding. It was first announced as a General Election commitment at the Conservative Party's annual Conference in September 2019 by the then Chancellor Sajid Javid.[32] Over five years from April 2020, it was to provide £560 million—that is, just over half of the £1.1 billion austerity cuts—to help local authorities' youth services in England '… build 60 new youth centres across the country, refurbish around 300 existing youth facilities, and provide over 100 mobile facilities for harder to reach areas'.[33]

Attributed in November 2020 to Covid and its impacts, a series of delays in its allocation then followed, generating disappointment and frustration in the field.[34] As by January 2021, only £30 million had been allocated just for 'capital spending', it had become clear that none of the

[29] Emily Harle, 2023, 'Youth work waiting lists soar amid financial pressures', *CYPN*, 18 September.

[30] Emily Harle, 2023, 'Youth organisations face changing landscape of residential schemes' *CYPN*, 30 August.

[31] Fiona Simpson, 2023, 'Sector hopes updated sufficiency rules will boost access to youth services', *CYPN*, 24 October.

[32] Joanne Parkes, 2019A, '"Javid announces £500m for youth fund"' *CYPN*, 30 September; Gov.UK, 2019, 'Chancellor announces support for post-Brexit future', 30 September, at https://www.gov.uk/government/news/chancellor-announces-support-for-post-brexit-future%2D%2D2#:~:text=A%20package%20of%20measures%20to,Javid%20today%20(30%20September).

[33] Rob Merrick, 2021, 'Hundreds of millions of pounds promised government cash for "collapsing" youth services shelved', *Independent*, 31 January.

[34] Joe Lepper, 2020, 'Urgent call for Youth Investment Fund "to stop sector collapse"', *CYPN*, 19 November.

money for actually running services was going to be available until April 2022. Especially given the new Covid pressures on government finances, this led to fears that the money might be used for other priorities, with the NYA's Chief Executive even suggesting that it had 'gone missing'.[35]

A month later, the then Youth Minister Baroness Barran did reaffirm the government's commitment to the Fund. However, in doing this, she announced that, rather than prioritising a reinstatement of year-round services, the money was to be used to 'support and drive innovation'.[36] By then, too, clarification of decisions on how what remained of the Fund's £560 million was to be spent was going to have to wait for the publication of the DCMS's report on a 'Youth Review' initiated by the Treasury in December 2020[37] (see Chap. 9). Finally released nine months after the promised date[38] via a process labelled at the time as 'money recycling', the YIF was in effect 're-launched' for the third time in February 2022.[39]

By then, underpinning the Fund was a government commitment to a National Youth Guarantee, also announced that month by the DCMS (see Chap. 9). As well as reiterating an intention to fund the Duke of Edinburgh Award Scheme (DoE) so that it was available in every state secondary school in England, the money was also to be used to support young people in employment.[40] In the context again of the government's 'levelling

---

[35] Rob Merrick, 2021, *Independent*, 31 January.

[36] Derren Hayes, 2021, 'Minister commits to Youth Investment Fund but focus will be on "innovation"', *CYPN*, 15 February.

[37] HM Treasury, 2020, 'Spending Review 2020: Executive Summary', updated 15 December, https://www.gov.uk/government/publications/spending-review-2020-documents/spending-review-2020.

[38] DCMS, 2022, *Youth Review: Summary findings and government response*, 1 February, 'Ministerial foreword', p. 3, https://www.gov.uk/government/publications/youth-review-summary-findings-and-government-response/youth-review-summary-findings-and-government-response.

[39] Fiona Simpson, 2021, 'Spending Review: Youth Investment Fund re-announced as part of £560m youth work boost', *CYPN*, 27 October.

[40] GOV.UK, 2022, 'Government announces ambitious plans to level up activities for young people', 1 February, https://www.gov.uk/government/news/government-outlines-ambitious-plans-to-level-up-activities-for-young-people, GOV.UK, 2022, 'Press release: £368 million fund to improve youth services in underserved areas open for bids', 1 August, https://www.gov.uk/government/news/368-million-fund-to-improve-youth-services-in-underserved-areas-opens-for-bids?utm_medium=email&utm_campaign=govuk-notifications-topic&utm_source=5810cbc6-db3b-43f8-a5d0-dd55e78b15f6&utm_content=weekly; Youth Investment Fund, 2022, 'About: What is the Youth Investment Fund?', 1 August, https://youthinvestmentfund.org.uk/about/; Joe Lepper, 2022, 'Government invites bids for share of £368m youth services fund', *CYPN*, 3 August.

up' policy, the new youth facilities were now also to be provided only in 'areas most in need'.

Nearly 30 per cent of £560 million (£171 million) remained earmarked for the NCS which—though now 'reformed', 'year round', focusing on local projects and with its peak annual funding cut by £9 million[41]—was still open only to 16- and 17-year-olds. Twenty-two million pounds was set aside for non-military Uniformed Youth Groups to 'eliminate current … waiting lists for teenagers up and down the country' and £4 million for an #iwill campaign which, Sajid Javid promised, would provide 'tens and thousands of new youth volunteering opportunities' (see Chap. 4).[42]

By May 2022, only £12 million of the Fund had actually been spent—'fast-tracked' to 418 youth projects for 'small-scale capital improvements such as providing new laptops to youth groups … and improving transport'. In August that year, with the £368 million still available ambitiously described by yet another new youth minister, Nigel Huddleston, as 'life-changing', a new round of bids was announced. This was still in part concentrated on refurbishing those 300 youth facilities—though, again, only if these were located in England's 600 most deprived wards in just 45 council areas. Over the next three years, the money would also have to ensure 'positive value', be used in ways which were 'environmentally sustainable' and 'enable positive activities for young people'.

A report released in September 2022 on how the Fund was then being used in the Yorkshire and Humberside region painted a far from positive picture of the realities on the ground. Though targeted at 'pockets of deprivation', these apparently often turned out to be in 'areas of greater wealth' rather than in those 'disadvantaged' areas which had experienced

[41] Fiona Simpson, 2022, 'NCS reveals details of year-round offer for 2023', *CYPN*, 15 November; Idox, 'National Citizens Service Launches 2023 Grants Programme', https://www.grantfinder.co.uk/national-citizens-service-launches-2023-grants-programme/, accessed 11 April 2023; DMU Consolation Group, 2023, 'The Future of Youth and Community Development at DMU', 11 April, p. 2, https://docs.google.com/document/d/10UKYP2dSW4ECaKdo4YngFsLOudZLs0y7jd5J57pa73c/edit; Joe Lepper, 2023, 'Revamped social action scheme sees NCS aim for great impact', *CYPN*, 3 January.

[42] DCMS, 2022, *Youth Review: Summary findings and government response*, 1 February, p. 4, https://www.gov.uk/government/publications/youth-review-summary-findings-and-government-response/youth-review-summary-findings-and-government-response.

a 'historic disinvestment in youth work' and an 'exodus of professional and skilled youth work staff'.[43]

This report appeared just before the release of two papers commissioned by the DCMS and produced by the market research company Ipsos UK.[44] The first—a 'process evaluation report' on YIF Phase 1—sought to inform the delivery of YIF Phase 2 by addressing three questions:

- 'What has worked well, and less well ...?'
- 'How far and in what ways did ... Phase 1 meet its objectives?'
- 'Demand for Phase 2'.

It also revealed that, with Phase 1 'substantially oversubscribed' by 1270 applications, the amount made available was increased from £10 million to £12 million, of which £11.7 million had by then been allocated for those 'small-scale capital projects' outlined above. This was then further explained as the '... urgent or shorter-term demand for equipment and/or capital that would enhance youth services, in particular digital infrastructure (a need highlighted by the pandemic)'.

The second paper explained a planned Ipsos 'impact evaluation feasibility study of (YIF) Phase 2' aimed at '... identify(ing) a range of design options for delivering a robust evaluation of the impact of Phase 2'. The first of its four chapters narrowed down a proposed 'theory of change' in part because its 'wide range of anticipated outcomes and impacts from the fund ... would not be practical or desirable ...'. Other chapters focused on a form of 'measurement of outcomes' which favoured a primary survey of youth organisations rather than of young people; on an 'impact evaluation recommendation' which 'constructs a comparison group made up of eligible organisations and areas that do not receive funding'; on 'the use of matching techniques and a difference-in-differences analysis'; and on 'approaches considered and rejected'.

A DCMS announcement in March 2023 eventually confirmed that 'youth services' in those approximately '600 districts and 45 local

---

[43] Joe Lepper, 2022, 'Deprived areas missing out on levelling up funding due to youth work spending differences, report finds', *CYPN*, 15 September.

[44] Ipsos UK, 2022, *Youth Investment Fund Phase 1: process evaluation report*, October, https://www.gov.uk/government/publications/youth-investment-fund-phase-1-process-evaluation; Ipsos UK, 2022, *Impact evaluation feasibility assessment of Phase 2 of Youth Investment Fund*, October, https://www.gov.uk/government/publications/youth-investment-fund-phase-2-impact-evaluation-feasibility-study.

authorities in England where the need was high and the provision low' were to share over £90 million of new YIF funding. These were the first grants from the Fund's second £300 million+ phase, intended 'to renew the country's youth sector' and so, in the words of Lucy Frazer, give '… every young person … the opportunity to access the kinds of life-changing activities which expand their horizons and allow them to develop vital life skills'.[45]

The following month (April 2023), a 'Refurbishment Grants Programme' was also launched. This sought bids of up to £150,000 'to ensure every eligible youth service can apply for funding to renovate their service' with the aim of increasing young people's participation in 'positive activities' in targeted areas by 45,000 a year.[46] This came with the announcement that, as the Fund would be closing in March 2025, all YIF-funded capital projects would have to be completed and all allocated monies spent before then, and that only applications for 'less complex, smaller projects' would now be considered.[47] In her speech to the YFF in October 2023, Lucy Frazer reported that

> … 87 organisations across the country have already received Youth Investment Fund money with over 200 more to come so we can provided safe spaces for young people … injecting £22 million directly to youth organisations in wards across England … identified as having high rates of antisocial behaviour.[48]

Despite the analysis (and rhetoric) of the Ipsos UK papers and the positive ministerial messages, the overall on-the-ground reality was that at best

[45] NYA, 2023, 'Youth Investment Fund of over £300 million allocated to first major beneficiaries to level up opportunities for young people', 27 March, https://www.nya.org.uk/yif-announcement/; Fiona Simpson, 2023, 'DCMS announces Youth Opportunities Fund recipients', CYPN, 28 March; Derren Hayes, 2023, 'Youth Investment Fund to boost vital support for young people', CYPN, 25 April.

[46] Youth Investment Fund, 2023, 'Refurbishment Grants Programme', Undated, https://youthinvestmentfund.org.uk/refurbishment-grants/https://youthinvestmentfund.org.uk/refurbishment-grants/, accessed 23 April 2023; Derren Hayes, 2023, 'Youth Investment Fund to boost vital support for young people', CYPN, 25 April.

[47] Youth Investment Fund, 2023, 'Changes to the Youth Investment Fund Grant Programme', 20 April, https://youthinvestmentfund.org.uk/news-insights/changes-to-the-youth-investment-fund-grant-programme/.

[48] GOV.UK, 2023, 'Lucy Frazer's speech at the Connected Futures conference', 12 October, https://www.gov.uk/government/speeches/lucy-frazers-speech-at-the-connected-futures-conference.

this remained a low government priority. A month after the Ipsos papers appeared, this was again highlighted by Chancellor Jeremy Hunt's Autumn 2022 Budget Statement which allocated billions of pounds over the following two years to schools and to children's and adult social care—but nothing to youth services.[49] In light of what was described as the 'challenging financial climate', his Budget the following March then actually cut £31 million from the YIF's £380 million previously promised for open youth work capital developments.[50] It also prompted a sharp critical response from the London Chamber of Commerce and Industry which claimed that, while London had been left out of the YIF funding allocations, the youth charity Onside had received £40 million to help develop its Youth Zones in a number of cities across England[51] (see Chap. 6). All this coincided, too, with confirmation of an extension of a DWP 'Youth Offer' for 16- to 24-year-olds to '… ensure that young people have the skills they need to look for, find and keep employment'.[52]

In August 2023, details were released of how the Phase 2 March and August 2023 YIF tranches had been allocated.[53] One hundred and sixty million pounds was being used to build new youth centres and refurbish old ones—such as Burnley Boys and Girls Club, to be 'transformed' with a grant of £974,000. The previous commitments remained, however, to the NCS and the Duke of Edinburgh Award Scheme, to creating new youth volunteering opportunities and to reducing uniformed organisations' waiting lists. Examples of the latter were an allocation of £1.8 million to a Sheffield Scout Group and money for the armed services' Cadet Force which, in its February 2022 'levelling up' White Paper, the

---

[49] Fiona Simpson, 2022, 'Autumn Statement: Jeremy Hunt announces funding for schools and children's social care', *CYPN*, 17 November.

[50] Lea Legraien, 2023, 'Youth Investment Fund cut by further £31m, DCMS confirms', *Civil Society*, 29 March.

[51] Joe Lepper, 2023, 'Business leaders challenge government over London youth services "funding snub"', *CYPN*, 4 May.

[52] Fiona Simpson, 2023, 'Budget 2023: Key announcements for children and young people', *CYPN*, 15 March; DWP, Undated, 'DWP Youth Offer', https://data.parliament.uk/DepositedPapers/Files/DEP2022-0452/179-Youth_Offer_V2.0.pdf.

[53] GOV.UK, 2023, 'Major boost for young people with plans to transform youth centres', https://www.gov.uk/government/news/major-boost-for-young-people-with-plans-to-transform-youth-centres#:~:text=New%20youth%20centres%20will%20be,of%20the%20Youth%20Investment%20Fund, 4 August.

government had described as a 'transformative opportunity' for school students[54] (see Chap. 9).

One consequence of the youth work sector's continuing uncertainties over funding was its increasing reliance on funding for voluntary organisations from the business world. In early 2023, for example, UK Youth announced a multi-million-pound fund using money donated by the Pears Foundation—a charity created by the billionaire owners of one of the UK's largest real estate companies.[55] On a visit to a youth club in Manchester two months earlier,[56] King Charles had given a high profile to the NatWest Bank's £3 million five-year funding for the NYA's 'Thrive' programme (see Chap. 7)[57]—to be used particularly to support practitioners get Level 3 or degree Level 6 leadership qualifications.[58] And in October, to fill a £1 million gap in funding for play and youth facilities in Bristol, a coalition of charities across the city called on local businesses to give financial support or share skills and services.[59]

Even with funding of this kind, however, the charitable sector overall continued to struggle, with many organisations by the end of 2023 still saying that they were on the brink of insolvency, not least because they were having to subsidise underfunded local authority contracts.[60]

[54] HM Government, 2022 'Levelling up in the United Kingdom: Executive Summary', February, p. 15, https://assets.publishing.service.gov.uk/government/uploads/system/uploads/attachment_data/file/1052046/Executive_Summary.pdf.

[55] Joe Lepper, 2023, 'Multi-million pound fund launches to support youth groups through the cost-of-living crisis', *CYPN*, 1 February; see also https://www.superyachtfan.com/yacht/talisman-c/owner/ accessed 4 March 2023.

[56] Emily Harle, 2023, 'King Charles visits youth club to mark funding boost for NYA programme', *CYPN*, 26 January.

[57] NYA, 2023, 'Further investment from NatWest to roll out NatWest Thrive', 23 January, https://www.nya.org.uk/further-investment-from-natwest-to-roll-out-natwest-thrive/.

[58] NYA, 2023, 'Free specialist skills offer', NYA email, 14 March; NYA, 2023, 'Apprentice funding scheme open', NYA email, 14 March; NYA, undated, 'Funding for apprentice training via NatWest Levy scheme', https://www.nya.org.uk/natwests-staff-volunteering-and-apprenticeship-levy-investment/.

[59] Joe Lepper, 2023, 'Charities urge local businesses to plug Bristol's £1m youth services gap', *CYPN*, 19 October.

[60] Patrick Butler, 2023, 'English charities "near insolvency" after subsidising public sector contracts', *Guardian*, 13 November.

# CHAPTER 4

# Open Youth Work: The Practice Evolves

**Abstract** Open youth work developments in this period took place in the context of a long-standing operational dilemma: from the 1960s, the significant national and local state resources on which the practice had come to rely often came with bureaucratic rules and procedures which could constrain its distinctive ways of working. With the Covid pandemic impacts creating a new ongoing context, key developments included

- NYA proposals to develop a youth work curriculum—an initiative which for managers and face-to-face practitioners within the sector created both possibilities and challenges.
- A renewed emphasis on 'youth voice', including by a government which said it 'want(ed) the next generation to be actively at the heart of our decision-making'.
- The prioritising of young people's volunteering, particularly through increased state funding for the '#iwill' and 'Step Up to Serve' campaign aimed at getting more young people involved in making a 'positive difference'.

**Keywords** State funding • Bureaucratic procedures • Youth work curriculum • 'Youth voice' • Youth volunteering

© The Author(s), under exclusive license to Springer Nature Switzerland AG 2024
B. Davies, *Youth Work Policies in England 2019–2023*,
https://doi.org/10.1007/978-3-031-65636-1_4

## STATE FUNDING—WITH STRINGS ATTACHED

Though, as evidenced in the last chapter, open youth work was never in this period a top government priority—and despite some significant budget cuts over the years—from the early 1960s through to the 2010s, the practice had drawn on significant amounts of state funding, both local and national. However, to get access to these resources, organisations, managers and face-to-face practitioners often had to negotiate complex bureaucratic procedures which were out of sync with the practice's declared aims and its process-led ways of working.[1]

These procedures did not go unchallenged. What, for example, in the UK became known as the 'Preston model' aimed to achieve 'a meaningful transfer of wealth and power back to local communities' in order to 'solv(e) problems from below without permission from above'.[2] More widely, however, the state's approaches to allocating its money could be very different. Organisations were often required to submit funding bids through complex commissioning procedures and, within tight time frames, then achieve 'outcomes' and 'impacts' imposed from above. As a result, many practitioners experienced the 'alienating effects of targets, intrusive (often statistical) monitoring and an over-emphasis on paperwork'.[3] With commissioning procedures often requiring bidders to treat each other as competitors, youth workers could also find themselves struggling to hold on to their preferred community-based and collaborative approaches.

## COVID, ITS IMPACTS—AND WIDER PRESSURES

As Covid took hold, the core day-to-day features of the practice also came under pressure. From very early in the pandemic, it was acknowledged that, long-term, the newer 'remote' ways of relating to young people could not be a substitute for those face-to-face encounters—young person with young person, young person with youth worker—which help define

[1] Bernard Davies, 2022, 'Manifesto for Youth Work: Some afterthoughts on the role of the state', *Youth and Policy*, May.

[2] Matthew Brown and Rhian E Jones, 2021, *Paint your Town Red: How Preston took back control and your town can do too*, Repeater Books, pp. 1, 2, 19.

[3] See, for example, Mark Smith, 2004, 'The case for youth work. Presentation to the Prime Minister's Strategy group', September', available at http://www.infed.org/archives/jeffs_and_smith/the_case_for_youth_work.html.

open youth work.[4] Nonetheless, to sustain these relationships while their buildings were closed, youth workers used digital methods in often highly creative ways, with detached and outreach projects also often re-thinking and extending their distinctive approaches.[5]

In partnership with the Open University and the Universities of Hull and Glasgow, the Professional Association of Lecturers in Youth and Community Work (PALYCW) sought through a 'research inquiry' to explore the effects of the pandemic on youth and community work.[6] Announced in February 2021 and set in the context of 'the new and persistent forms of social injustice and inequalities that impact young people …', its remit was to examine 'the changing nature of youth and community work practice and the entanglements with teaching practices in and across professionally qualifying youth and community work programmes'. This was to be done by capturing youth and community work lecturers' teaching experiences during the pandemic in order to 'look forward to the future post-pandemic (whenever that might be)'.

As the evidence built of how damaging this was for young people, the ten youth organisations of the Back Youth Alliance sent an open letter to the press arguing for greater state support for open youth work.[7] Though in January 2021, the government did give the practice more formal recognition by designating it a 'key front-line service' being delivered by 'key workers',[8] much (most) of its financial support remained constrained within the forms of targeted 'gesture' funding discussed in Chap. 3.

---

[4] Graham Duxbury, 2020, 'Why we can't Zoom our way of the C19 crisis', *CYPN*, 27 May.

[5] Fiona Simpson, 2020, 'Youth work services move online to protect vulnerable children', *CYPN*, 17 April; Graeme Tiffany, 2022, 'COVID19 as a potentially valuable disruptive force in the conceptualisation of Street-based Youth Work', 28 January, https://www.youthand-policy.org/articles/covid19-as-a-potentially-valuable-disruptive/; Nina Jacobs, 2023, 'Detached youth work engages young people in their own spaces', *CYPN*, 24 October; Derren Hayes, 2023, 'Access to Youth Work: Special Report', *CYPN*, 24 October; NYA, 2023, *The social cost of youth work cuts: Preventing youth offending through youth work*, November, https://www.nya.org.uk/youth-work-and-crime/#:~:text=youth%20work%20saves%20%C2%A3500,3.20%20%E2%80%93%20%C2%A36.40%20of%20value.

[6] PALYCW, 2021, 'Research Inquiry: Reimagining our future – youth and community work education during and post Covid-19', Members' Email, 5 February.

[7] See, for example, Back Youth Alliance, 2020, 'Harnessing the power of the youth sector in the Covid-19 crisis – an Open Letter to Government', 20 March, https://www.ukyouth.org/2020/03/harnessing-the-power-of-the-youth-sector-in-the-covid-19-crisis-an-open-letter-to-government/.

[8] Fiona Simpson, 2021, 'Youth workers given key worker status', *CYPN*, 8 January.

Very quickly, the pressures on youth work provision were further revealed. By mid-2020, it was being reported that many youth work facilities were threatened with permanent closure,[9] including within the voluntary youth sector (see Chap. 6); that at least 300,000 young people were no longer being 'reached' by 'youth work services';[10] and, by being forced 'off the radar', that an estimated over one million were no longer accessing any form of youth service provision or activities.[11] Two years later (in October 2022), after nearly a decade and a half of advocating for open youth work practice and provision, In Defence of Youth Work concluded that it had 'run its course' and closed down as a campaigning group.[12] By then, too, youth work providers were finding it difficult to recruit both qualified youth workers and also—as the cost-of-living crisis took hold—volunteers[13] (see Chap. 8).

That open youth work was still a low government priority was again at least implicitly illustrated in November 2022 by its location of the 'youth minister' role within a wide portfolio covering sport, tourism, the Eurovision Song Contest—and the King's coronation.[14] Long-time youth work commentator Tony Jeffs also raised a more fundamental doubt about the practice's role—suggesting that its overall reach '… had largely become a myth, with most projects now catering to younger (under 14) age groups'.[15]

[9] Derren Hayes, 2020, 'Lockdown restrictions threaten youth groups' future', *CYPN*, 28 May; Derren Hayes, Ella Doyle and Isabella McRae, 2021, 'Lockdown response: how services deliver vital support for children', *CYPN*, 26 January.

[10] Fiona Simpson, 2020, '3000,000 young people missing out on youth work services, analysis finds', *CYPN*, 17 June.

[11] Nina Jacobs, 2020, 'NYA calls for youth workers in every secondary school catchment area', *CYPN*, 21 July.

[12] Joe Lepper, 2022, 'Youth work campaign groups closes after "losing its impetus and energy"', *CYPN*, 12 October.

[13] Emily Harle, 2023 'Youth work waiting lists soar amid financial pressures, report finds', *CYPN*, 18 September; Emily Harle, 2023, 'Youth organisations face changing landscape of residential schemes', *CYPN*, 30 August; Andrew Hanna, undated, 'Volunteering: The Impact of the Cost-of-Living Crisis', *Volunteering Now*, accessed 29 November 2023, https://www.volunteernow.co.uk/volunteering-the-impact-of-the-cost-of-living-crisis/#:~:text=Volunteer%20Now%20is%20currently%20undertaking,(VCS)%20as%20a%20whole.

[14] Joe Lepper, 2022, 'Stuart Andrew takes on youth minister role', *CYPN*, 9 November.

[15] Tony Jeffs, 2022, 'The Youth Work Myth', *Youth and Policy*, April, https://www.youthandpolicy.org/articles/youth-work-myth/.

By then, too, a wider debate had been going on for some years on how best to provide 'youth work' and improve young people's access to it, including by locating it in a much wider range of agencies (see Chap. 5). For Ann Longfield, the Chair of the Commission on Young Lives and a former Children's Commissioner for England, the priority was to develop youth hubs linked to schools—identified also by some as a way of bringing together services tackling youth violence (see Chap. 5). On the other hand, NYA's Director of Youth Work, Abbee McLatchie, continued to favour facilities which, purpose-built and community-based, could make 'a really holistic offer for (those) young people not necessarily … well engaged in school' and for whom 'school may not feel like a safe place …'.[16]

By late 2023, in a 'special report' on access to youth work published by *Children and Young People Now* (CYPN), some 'green shoots of recovery' were identified—prompted particularly by the government's promise through the YIF to 'invest' in 300 new youth centres (see Chap. 3) and to fund training bursaries for support workers (see Chap. 8).[17] However, the report's appearance coincided with the launch of a *Roadmap to a National Youth Strategy* by the National Youth Sector Advisory Board (NYSAB)—a coalition of 20 youth sector organisations including the NYA.[18] This saw a need for the government to improve young people's access to 'quality youth work' through, for example, 'long-term and increased financial investment' and an 'increased, professionalised and diverse youth work-force'. Specific focuses for the practice were also identified, including 'reduced crime, with young people safe from harm', 'facilitating, developing and empowering young people's voice and influence' and addressing their growing mental health needs.

It was within these wider, often constraining, conditions that open youth work practice struggled to operate in this period.

---

[16] Derren Hayes, 2023, 'Access to Youth Work: Special Report', *CYPN*, 24 October; Derren Hayes, 2023, 'The Big Debate: What is the key to improving access to youth work services?', *CYPN*, 24 October.

[17] Derren Hayes, 2023, 'Access to Youth Work: Special Report', *CYPN*, 24 October.

[18] NYA, 2023, *Roadmap to National Youth Strategy*, October, https://s3.eu-west-1.amazonaws.com/assets.nya2.joltrouter.net/wp-content/uploads/2023/11/01165048/Roadmap-to-national-youth-strategy-DIGITAL.pdf, Joe Lepper, 2023, 'Roadmap to improve youth services launches,', *CYPN*, 4 October.

## A Curriculum For Youth Work

One initiative intended to support and help clarify its role—the development of an explicit youth work curriculum—had a long back story. In 1989, Conservative 'youth minister' Alan Howarth had made an in effect neo-liberal case for a lack of cohesion' in local authority Youth Services[19] by, in explicitly 'commercial terms', proposing a 'national curriculum' for youth work. To implement this, he suggested, required 'finding a gap in the market, identifying the service needed, assessing consumer demand or need, finding backers and providing evidence of effective delivery'.[20]

During the 1990s, the government increased its pressure on local authority Youth Services to introduce a curriculum; despite some initial resistance, 77 per cent had adopted one by the end of the decade.[21] Though this had not given open youth work facilities any discernible protection from the austerity cuts, in September 2020, NYA used these to justify the launch of a revised and detailed 'Curriculum for Youth Work' (see Chap. 7). Significantly, however, by the end of 2023, government publications such as the guidance paper for the YIF (see Chap. 3) and the DCMS's *Youth Review* report (see Chap. 9) were making no reference to it or to why it was needed.[22]

## 'Youth Voice'

One form of response to young people which did get government and wider encouragement in this period also had a long history within open youth work: a commitment to young people both shaping the aims and

[19] Jackie Scott, 1990, 'Strength through diversity', *Young People Now*, No 15, July, p 36. See also Jon Ord, 'The Youth Work Curriculum and the "Transforming Youth Work Agenda"', https://www.researchgate.net/profile/Jon-Ord-2/publication/311518927_The_Youth_Work_Curriculum_the_Transforming_Youth_Work_Agenda/links/584a913a08aedf2b6e98db93/The-Youth-Work-Curriculum-the-Transforming-Youth-Work-Agenda.pdf.

[20] Alan Howarth, 1989, *Towards a Core Curriculum for the Youth Service: Report of the First Ministerial Conference*, 'Keynote Address', National Youth Bureau, Paras 7, 13, 26, 37.

[21] Bernard Davies, 2008, *The New Labour Years: A History of the Youth Service in England Vol 3, 1997–2007*, NYA, p. 144.

[22] See, for example, GOV.UK, 2022, '£368 million fund to improve youth services in underserved areas opens for bids', 1 August, https://www.gov.uk/government/news/368-million-fund-to-improve-youth-services-in-underserved-areas-opens-for-bids#:~:text=Press%20release-,%C2%A3368%20million%20fund%20to%20improve%20youth,underserved%20areas%20opens%20for%20bids&text=Youth%20services%20in%20the%20country's,and%20opportunities%20for%20young.

programmes of the practice itself and acting to influence wider societal policies and provision affecting them and their generation. This commitment was reaffirmed when the state became directly involved in providing open youth work—for example, in the government circulars which created the Service of Youth in 1939/1940 and in later Youth Service review reports.[23] In the context of a proposed revision of the statutory guidance on local authority Youth Services (see Chap. 9), the then Children's Minister Tim Loughton talked in 2012 of 'want(ing) to give young people the keys to the town hall so their views drive what services are funded for them and they can inspect their quality'.[24]

As something of a corrective to this kind of rhetoric, as far back as 1991, an independent report on the management of Youth Services in England had concluded that 'the participation of young people in the planning process (was) ... a neglected aspect' of its work on which 'few LEAs seem to have made much progress ...'.[25] Perhaps with this as a prompt, in the later 1990s and into the 2000s, New Labour governments had made young people's 'participation' a high-profile objective—expressed, for example, in its creation of a Youth Parliament and of Youth Capital and Youth Opportunities Funds which gave young people significant say in how some local funds were allocated.

In a sub-section of its 2011 policy paper *Positive for Youth* headed 'Promoting youth voice', the Conservative-Liberal Democrat Coalition government also embraced the aim of '... empowering young people ... to inspect and report on local services and ... help "youth proof" government policy'. This was to include ministers working with and through the Youth Parliament and the British Youth Council (BYC)[26]—an aspiration reaffirmed in August 2020 by the 'youth minister' Baroness Barran when

[23] Board of Education. 1939, *Circular 1486 – the service of youth'*, Appendix para 2; Board of Education. 1940, *The Challenge of Youth* (Circular 1516), 27 June, para 7; Albemarle Report, 1960, *The Youth Service in England and Wales*, HMSO, p. 48; Fairbairn-Milson Report, 1969, *Youth and Community Work in the 70s*, London, HMSO, para 195; Thompson Report, 1982, *Experience and Participation: Report of the Review Group on the Youth Service in England*, HMSO, para 5.17.

[24] Neil Puffett, 2012, 'Young voices must be heard in decisions on youth service provision, says DfE', *CYPN*, 5 March.

[25] Department of Education and Science, 1991, 'Managing the Youth Service in the 1990s', May, para 318.

[26] HM Government, 2011, *Positive for Youth: A New Approach to Government Policy for Young People Aged 13 to 19*, Executive Summary, para 6.12, 6.13, p 88; Andy Hillier, 2011, 'Young people will have a say in government's youth policy, says Loughton', *CYPN*, 10 March.

she talked of '… listening carefully to young people' and '… want(ing) the next generation to be actively at the heart of our decision-making'.[27]

By then, the BYC was managing 'Involved', an Instagram website which, via 'opinion polls and cross-government consultations on the latest hot topics', invited young people's views and comments to 'be shared anonymously with the Department for Digital, Culture, Media and Sport'. By early November 2020, the site had attracted over 1150 followers and had fed back to ministers on youth violence, volunteering and 'youth services'.[28]

As evidence emerged that, because they were participating less in politics than any other age group young people could have been suffering materially,[29] it became clear that the harder realities of government policies could often fail to match its 'youth voice' claims. This had been demonstrated in 2010 when, without consultation with young people, the Coalition government had cut the Youth Capital Fund budget by half.[30] Against the background of huge overall reductions in the Treasury's financial support for local authorities, it then removed the ringfencing of the money for this and for the Youth Opportunity Fund which had resulted in both being wound up within months.[31]

Other examples of the gap between government 'youth voice' rhetoric and its practice included

[27] Baroness Barran, 2020, 'Youth Minister: Young people have a key role to play in our nation's recovery', *CYPN*, 20 August.

[28] Instagram, 2020, 'Involved UK', https://www.instagram.com/involved. uk/?igshid=f64mcwwo7yvw. See also British Youth Council, 2020, 'You are the voice of the future', https://www.byc.org.uk/involved; both accessed 18 October 2020; Fiona Simpson, 2020, '#Chances4children: young people to influence Covid-19 policy using Instagram', *CYPN*, 3 July.

[29] Behavioural Insights Team, 2021, *Getting young people into politics through service learning*, 8 December, https://www.bi.team/publications/getting-young-people-into-politics-through-service-learning/.

[30] For example, Youth Association, 2010, 'LS $ash', 14 October, http://youth-association. org/tag/youth-capital-fund/.

[31] Andy Hillier, 2010, 'Youth Opportunity Fund at risk as ringfence expected to go', *CYPN*, 7 June.

- Education Secretary Michael Gove's insistence in 2013 that, despite young people's opposition,[32] responsibility for youth policy be moved out of his department.
- Again without consultation, and with stressful consequences for many young people and for the education system overall,[33] Gove's radical reform of the content and format of the GCSE and A level examinations—a move which in December 2023 a House of Lords report recommended should be reversed.[34]
- Prime Minister Sunak and his ministers' impositions of new limitations on the range and curricula of higher education courses in England, with potentially damaging consequences particularly for working class and Black, Asian and minority applicants.[35]

A commitment to ensuring a youth voice in policy-making was however restated in July 2022 when the DCMS announced a six-month extension of its funding for the Shout Out UK youth policy development group. Launched in 2021 by a social enterprise set up six years earlier, this aimed to 'fix the lack of political education in schools by bringing young people together'.[36]

Other non-government groups also continued to work to strengthen the 'youth voice' influence. To mark its 40th anniversary in November 2022, for example, Groundwork, a charity committed to community action on poverty and the environment, announced plans for greater youth engagement focused on climate change and the cost-of-living crisis.[37] By then, in August 2022, the #iwill youth volunteering project

[32] Neil Puffett, 2013, 'Young people to probe Gove's dismissal of youth policy' *CYPN*, 8 February; Neil Puffett, 2013, 'Young people call on Gove to invest in youth services', *CYPN*, 11 February.

[33] See, for example, Sally Weale, 2018, 'Stress and serious anxiety: how the new GCSE is affecting mental health', *Guardian*, 17 May; Polly Toynbee, 2023, 'Too many pupils miss lessons, says Ofsted, and that's right. Call it the Michael Gove effect', *Guardian*, 28 November.

[34] Sally Weale, 2023, 'Peers call for urgent overhaul of secondary education in England', *Guardian*, 12 December.

[35] Richard Adams, Aubrey Allegretti, ' Sunak to force English universities to cap numbers of students on "low value" degrees', *Guardian*, 14 July.

[36] Fiona Simpson, 2022, 'DCMS announces funding extension for youth policy development group', *CYPN*, 6 July.

[37] Emily Harle, 2022, Charity reveals aims to boost youth engagement in social action', *CYPN*, 17 November.

(discussed below) had drawn on insights from a data trawl showing that in the programmes it was funding:

> ... *the most common type of activities to enable youth voice at programme level are young people's advisory groups (25%), followed by young people co-designing/ leading programme development (16%) and young people being involved as members of decision-making bodies (16%).*[38]

A year later, it published a further analysis of this data in a report, *Establishing Youth Voice*,[39] which also drew on responses from 70 workshop participants, including some who were members of its Young Evaluators Panel. This provided detailed evidence and conclusions on, for example, how 'youth voice' was happening in practice, what was enabling and what was inhibiting this practice, the difference 'youth voice' activities were making and the implications of these findings for policy-makers, funders, practitioners, 'delivery organisations' and communities.

Launched in 2022 by the YMCA George Williams College in collaboration with the Centre for Youth Impact (CYI) and other organisations, a 'Maximising Young People's Voice and Power' project focused more specifically on developing 'a typology of youth voice practice'.[40] Its 'four key ambitions' were to 'better understand current youth voice activity in the UK ...', 'ensure more young people ... are heard and have influence in decision making processes', 'enhance equity' and 'improve access to information'. One of the project's Steering Group sessions also agreed a definition of 'youth voice' which, published in a November 2022 paper, advocated

---

[38] Centre for Youth Impact, 2022, 'Insights From the Data Trawl on Youth Voice Practice', 16 August, https://www.youthimpact.uk/latest/news/insights-data-trawl-youth-voice-practice.

[39] Tom Burke et al, 2023, *Establishing Youth Voice,* #iwill, August, https://www.ymca-georgewilliams.uk/sites/default/files/2023-08/EYV%20Final%20Report%20FINAL%20 3.0.pdf.

[40] YMCA George Williams College, 2022, 'Let's talk about youth voice: why is it important?', 18 November, https://www.ymcageorgewilliams.uk/latest/news/lets-talk-about-youth-voice-why-it-important#:~:text=As%20part%20of%20the%20Maximising,the%20 umbrella%20of%20youth%20voice. See also YMCA George Williams College, undated', Youth Voice, Influence and Power', https://www.ymcageorgewilliams.uk/our-projects/ Youth-Voice-Influence-and-Power,accessed 4 December 2023.

*Providing support (i.e. the space, skills and time) for young people to express their views and ideas, and action being taken based on what they say. This practice will result in positive change, in the situation, context or organisation that the young person is sharing their views about (e.g. the services they or others receive), in the young person's personal development, or both.*

The session also agreed that 'youth voice' was important both '... because it supports young people to … have an impact' and 'in making sure organisations have a realistic and accurate understanding of young people's views'. It thus recommended that

*… all organisations working with young people should invest time and resource in providing spaces for young people to express their views and ideas, and take action based on what is shared.*

Through the BYC, the DCMS continued to provide funding for the Youth Parliament—by then made up of 300 elected members aged between 11 and 18. After allocating £233,000 in 2021–22, following a review of its youth engagement strategy in November 2022, it announced a 'relaunch' of the programme.[41] This coincided with a Youth Parliament decision to campaign in the coming year on the cost-of-living crisis and health issues.[42] A further increase in DCMS funding, confirmed in March 2023, brought commitments of up to £650,000 for core costs, up to £100,000 to ensure young people from the devolved nations could participate and a further £10,000 to enable BYC to continue running a Youth Select Committee to scrutinise relevant government policies.[43]

A report released early in 2023 offered some insight into how closely these 'youth voice' initiatives were aligned with young people's own expectations and proposals and the influence they were having on

[41] Emily Harle, 2022, 'UK Youth Parliament tender bids to expand reach of programme', *CYPN*, 1 December.

[42] Emily Harle, 2022, 'UK Youth Parliament votes to campaign on cost of living and health', *CYPN*, 9 November.

[43] Fiona Simpson, 2023, 'British Youth Council wins £750k grant to run UK Youth Parliament', *CYPN*, 10 March; GOV.UK, 2023, 'UK Youth Parliament Grant awarded to the British Youth Council', 8 March, https://www.gov.uk/government/news/uk-youth-parliament-grant-awarded-to-the-british-youth-council#:~:text=The%20Department%20 for%20Culture%2C%20Media,Parliament%20Grant%20for%202023%2D25.

ministerial decisions. It was produced by the Peer Action Collective[44] which had been brought together by the Youth Endowment Fund, the #iwill Fund and the Co-op group. Describing itself as 'a ground-breaking network of Peer Researchers and Changemakers', the report started from the proposition that

> *All too often, young people who experience violence aren't heard, and are not seen as co-producers of social action and change to create safer and fairer communities.*

By the time the paper appeared, the Collective was reporting that it had 'involved over **6000** young people in research and social action … (for) making their worlds a safer place'.

However, the findings of a broader study of 'youth engagement' led by Ecorys UK and Participation People, published in July 2023, raised doubts about the effectiveness of the UK Parliament and the Youth Policy Development Group. Based on interviews and focus group discussions with participants and non-participants and also with policy-makers, it revealed significant limitations in how young people were informed and recruited, which groups therefore actually became involved and which felt (or were) excluded.[45]

It was against this background of mixed messages about the realities of 'youth voice' in action that in September 2023, in the run-up to the anticipated 2024 General Election, the Children's Commissioner for England, Rachel de Souza, announced a Big Ambition campaign aimed at consulting 6- to 18-year-olds on their political priorities. Drawing on a survey which had already been sent to 22,500 schools, the findings were to be used to encourage policy-makers to consider the needs of those who were too young to vote.[46]

---

[44] Peer Action Collective, 2022, *Leading Research, Driving Change: Youth insights and solutions from the Peer Action Collective,* Youth Endowment Fund, undated, https://youthendowmentfund.org.uk/peer-action-collective/.

[45] GOV.UK, 2023, *Youth engagement impact study: youth summary,* 12 July, https://www.gov.uk/government/publications/youth-engagement-impact-study/youth-engagement-impact-study-youth-summary; Emily Harle, 2023, 'UKYP needs better promotion to broaden reach, study finds', *CYPN,* 24 July.

[46] Emily Harle, 2023, 'Children's commissioner seeks young people's views ahead of the general election', *CYPN,* 14 September.

## YOUTH VOLUNTEERING

Though extending youth volunteering opportunities was clearly an important element of its 'youth voice' initiatives, their encouragement by the government went much further. Its financial and other support for the NCS in 2022–23, for example, enabled the Scheme through its 'Changemakers' projects to involve nearly 9400 young people in 73,474 hours of social action and volunteering activities.[47]

### *#iwill: Step Up to Serve—And Beyond*

Most high profile in providing these opportunities, however, was the '#iwill campaign'. Following an 'independent review' set up with cross-party support by the then Prime Minister David Cameron, this had been launched in November 2013 by the then Prince of Wales and co-ordinated initially by the charity Step Up to Serve.[48] As this was due to close by the end of 2020, in October of that year, expressions of interest were invited from organisations willing to take on key support functions up to 2025 to sustain what by then had become an #iwill 'movement'.[49] The chosen organisation(s) would be required to act as 'a central co-ordinating hub' and as 'delivery partners' to manage the #iwill Ambassador & Champion Network and 'gather evidence and insights to shape collective action'.

For making progress towards what it labelled 'shared Impact Goals', the Expression of Interest' document also made explicit the need for 'more organisations—and the decision-makers who lead them—(to) … work in partnership with young people to solve common challenges'. To help achieve this, a 'Power of Youth Charter' was launched—described as 'a framework to empower more young people to make a positive difference'—and a new 'Power of Youth Index' was created to enable organisations to assess how they were doing this.

[47] NCS Trust, 2023, *Annual Report 2022–23*, DCMS, 7 December, https://assets.publishing.service.gov.uk/media/6572e6c233b7f20012b720c6/E03008536_National_Citizen_Service_Trust_ARA_22-23_Web_Accessible.pdf.

[48] Step Up to Serve Newsletter, 2017, 'Leaders renew cross-party support for #iwill', 20 Nov; Cleverdon, J., and Jordan, A., 2012, *In the Service of Others: A vision for youth social action by 2020*, December, https://www.gov.uk/government/uploads/system/uploads/attachment_data/file/211937/In_the_Service_of_Others_-_A_vision_for_youth_social_action_by_2020.pdf.

[49] Step Up to Serve, 2020, 'Delivery support functions for #iwill beyond 2020: Expressions of Interest Information Document', October.

With the overall aspiration of 'encourag(ing) 1.7 million more young people to make helping others a habit for life', in January 2021, the lead organisational role was taken on by UK Youth and Volunteering Matters.[50] The following month, the new interim co-chairs set out #iwill's 'broader goals' which included 'a greater focus on supporting young people from low-income backgrounds and Black and ethnic minority groups'.[51] Through its now 400 active young Ambassadors and Champions, #iwill also sought to lay foundations 'to transform the role and perception of children and young people within society' by, across the UK, 'convening and connecting, communicating with and challenging' over a thousand 'pledge partners'.[52]

In August 2021, Baroness Barran announced an additional £4 million for International Youth Day. This was followed a year later by a joint allocation with the National Lottery of £12 million for 'youth social action' so that by August 2022, their funding for #iwill totalled £66 million.[53]

In June 2023, #iwill celebrated the tenth anniversary of its creation through a 'Power of Youth Day' whose theme—'This Is Me'—focused on four questions to be explored by young people, supporters and partners. These included 'Are you including young people in board meetings or decision-making forums?' and 'Are you creating conditions for young people to explore new ways to shape change?'[54] Also focused on marking the anniversary was '#iwill Week', its 'annual celebration of the work young people, Ambassadors, Champions and partners are leading up and

[50] UK Youth, 2021, 'UK Youth and Volunteering Matters to deliver key support functions of the #iwill Partnership and movement', 28 January, https://www.ukyouth.org/2021/01/uk-youth-and-volunteering-matters-form-consortium-to-deliver-key-support-functions-of-the-iwill-partnership-and-movement/.

[51] Tom McEachan and Dame Julia Claverdon, 2021, 'Collaboration at the heart', email dated 3 February.

[52] #iwill, 'About us', https://www.iwill.org.uk/about-us, accessed 10 December 2020; See also: Step Up to Serve, 2020, 'Delivery support functions for #iwill beyond 2020', https://www.iwill.org.uk/wp-content/uploads/2020/10/iwill-EOI-Information-Doc-201005.pdf.

[53] Derren Hayes, 2022, 'Youth social action gets funding boost' *CYPN*, 8 July; Fiona Simpson, 2021, 'International Youth Day: #iwill fund to receive £4m investment to support social action projects', *CYPN*, 12 August; National Lottery, 2022, '£12 million #iwill Fund boost to support youth social action across the country', https://www.tnlcommunityfund.org.uk/news/press-releases/2022-07-07/12-million-iwill-fund-boost-to-support-youth-social-action-across-the-country, 7 July.

[54] #iwill email, 2023, 'It's Power of Youth Day', 6 June.

down the UK'. As a prompt for 'imagin(ing) what the next decade will look like for youth social action', over seven days young people and #iwill partners hosted online and in-person events to explore 'the next big thing'. Sessions included a workshop on 'Removing barriers to youth social action', a preview of a film made by an #iwill Ambassador, and 'Deaf Awareness' training.[55]

### *Aspirations, Aims—And Take-up*

For the 2020 *Summary Report* of Ipsos MORI's annual evaluation,[56] Step Up to Serve defined 'meaningful' social action as

> ... *those who have participated at least every few months over the last 12 months ... or been involved in a one-off activity lasting more than a day; and (who) recognise that their activities had some benefit for both themselves and others.*

It also explained the practice of volunteering as

> ... *a wide range of activities that help other people or the environment, such as fundraising, campaigning, tutoring/mentoring and giving time to charity.*

The 2020 report recorded a rise in involvement in 'campaigning/raising awareness' from 8 per cent in 2017 and 2018 to 12 per cent in 2019.[57] Explicitly drawing on 'a classification of social action activities used by Step Up To Serve', an evaluation of the Uniformed Youth Social Action Fund in 2016 explained campaigning activities as 'primarily related to Remembrance Day activities, such as 'parades' and that 'in the social action context (this) is always non-political'.[58] These, however, remained

[55] #iwill email, 4 November 2023; #iwill Movement, 2023, '#iwill Week', https://www.iwill.org.uk/iwill-week-events/?utm_source=All+Contacts&utm_campaign=53e34dc451-EMAIL_CAMPAIGN_2022_11_29_02_25_COPY_01&utm_medium=email&utm_term=0_-c4853eb72b-%5BLIST_EMAIL_ID%5D, accessed 6 December 2023.

[56] Yota Bratsa, Claudia Mollidor, Jane Stevens, 2020, *National Youth Social Action Survey 2019: Summary Report*, Ipsos MORI, May. See also Fiona Simpson, 2020, 'Social action: Step Up to Serve fails to reach most disadvantaged young people', *CYPN*, 24 November.

[57] IpsosMORI, 2020, National Youth Social Action Survey;16 November, https://www.ipsos.com/en-uk/national-youth-social-action-survey.

[58] Ilana Tyler-Rubinstein, Fiona Vallance, Olivia Michelmore and Julia Pye, 2016, *Evaluation of the Unformed Youth Social Action Fund 1: Final Report,* Ipsos Mori, October 2016, p. 5, 46. Campaigning in the social action context is always non-political.(46).

a minority activity alongside 'fundraising or a sponsored event' in which 43 per cent of young people took part in 2015–18 and 39 per cent in 2019.[59]

For a heavily state-funded organisation like Step Up to Serve, focusing on de-politicised versions of social action like these may well have been unavoidable. This, however, contrasted sharply with the more radical approaches explicitly defined as 'collective action' which over this period were adopted by, for example, Greta Thunberg and Extinction Rebellion and by the Black Lives Matter movement. Moreover, though Step Up to Serve did reference 'the climate emergency' and 'racial injustice' as 'unprecedented … challenges', the nearest it came to recognising how deeply these might be embedded in society's political and economic power structures was when it acknowledged that 'the consequences of meaningful power-sharing will be challenging and change-making (otherwise what's the point)?'.[60]

The findings of the 2020 Ipsos MORI report on young people's overall participation in volunteering revealed that between 2015 and 2019, this had fallen from 59 to 53 per cent, with their involvement in what it called 'meaningful' social action also falling, from 42 to 36 per cent.[61] In the 12 months after 2018, other evidence emerged that 'young people from the poorest backgrounds tended to be the least likely to access structured social action opportunities'.[62] Though the 'participation gap' between the most and the least affluent closed slightly (from 14 to 12 percentage points), it nonetheless remained significant, with only 29 per cent of participants defined as 'C2DEs' compared with 41 per cent as 'ABC1'.

The report also found that, compared with 12 per cent in 2018 and only 4 per cent in 2017, in 2019, 19 per cent of young people felt there

[59] IpsosMORI, 2020, National Youth Action Survey;16 November, https://assets.publishing.service.gov.uk/media/5f9b19a3d3bf7f1e4249b3a6/National_Youth_Social_Action_Survey_2019_-_Summary_Report-c.pdf.

[60] James Cathcart, 2020, 'The power of youth, from silent service to youth voice leadership', *CYPN*, 18 February, https://www.cypnow.co.uk/blogs/article/the-power-of-youth-from-silent-service-to-youth-voice-leadership.

[61] Yota Bratsa, Claudia Mollidor, Jane Stevens, 2020, *National Youth Social Action Survey 2019: Summary Report*, Ipsos MORI, May. See also Fiona Simpson, 2020, 'Social action: Step Up to Serve fails to reach most disadvantaged young people', *CYPN*, 24 November.

[62] Steve Holliday, 2018, *Independent review of Full-time Social Action*, January, https://assets.publishing.service.gov.uk/government/uploads/system/uploads/attachment_data/file/679078/The_Steve_Holliday_Report.pdf, p. 2.

were 'few/no (volunteering) opportunities in my area'.[63] This was supported in September 2022 by an Institute for Community Studies finding that in rural areas young people had fewer of these opportunities anyway, prompting it to recommend the need for '... a common language for youth volunteering ...' and for '... youth-centred pathways in the "volunteering journey"'.[64]

The Ipsos MORI survey also found that in 2019, only 50 per cent of the young people responding believed the wider public took their participation in social action seriously, with the proportion between 2016 and 2018 who felt their efforts were being recognised falling from 60 to 54 per cent. Despite this, 88 per cent of the young people surveyed said they still 'cared about making the world a better place' and 74 per cent felt 'they could make a difference'.

### ... And Impacts: Actual and Intended

Though often not by a majority, many young people also recognised a range of personal gains. These included 'increased self-confidence/self-esteem' (mentioned by 44 per cent); 'improved communication skills' (42 per cent), improvements in 'how you work as part of a team' (38 per cent) and 'improved social skills' (31 per cent). Re-interpreted as 'character development', The Challenge, one of the organisations central to the delivery of NCS, pointed to similar outcomes as particularly important for helping NEET young people get 'back on track'.[65] This view was supported by the findings of a later survey—that, for example, 73 per cent of the 16–19-year-old respondents credited volunteering with improving their job prospects.[66]

For the government, other motivations—here, too, often framed by neo-liberal ideas—drove the #iwill 'investment', with a 2017 report, for example, arguing that 'a national full-time volunteering programme ...

[63] Yota Bratsa, Claudia Mollidor, Jane Stevens, 2020, *National Youth Social Action Survey 2019: Summary Report*, Ipsos MORI, p. 5, May.

[64] Fiona Simpson, 2022,'Young people offered fewer volunteering opportunities in rural areas', *CYPN*, 20 September.

[65] Nina Jacobs, 2019, 'Character development scheme targets those at NEET risk', *CYPN*, 29 October.

[66] Stephen Delahunty, 2021, 'High proportion of young people credit volunteering with helping then find work, research shows', *Third Sector*, 29 April.

could boost the UK economy by up to £199m a year'.[67] Despite, two months later, an 'independent' review concluding that 'the evidence base relating to full-time social action is not strong enough at present to recommend legislative change to widen access',[68] in its September 2020 *Levelling up Our Communities*[69] paper the government endorsed the notion of 'paid volunteering'. It specifically recommended 'a structured programme' to 'subsidise under-employed young people to work on a range of social and environmental projects' through which they could 'serve their local areas in meaningful roles that build their skills and their sense of public duty'. The report also suggested the programme be linked to the government's Kickstart scheme for supporting the wages of 350,000 young people employed mainly in the private sector.[70]

With the aim of increasing 'youth employability', in October 2023, the DCMS allocated £1 million to the NCS's UK Year of Service programme to fund a more focused approach to opening up such opportunities. Following a three-year pilot to support 336 young people into employment, the new scheme was to provide 100 18- to 24-year-olds with placements in community-based projects, further skills training and support after the scheme finished.[71]

## OPEN YOUTH WORK IN 2023

All three of the practice areas discussed in this chapter—a youth work curriculum, 'youth voice' and youth volunteering—clearly have strong content- and activity-focuses. From an open youth work perspective, two questions therefore merit some further critical and evidenced response:

[67] Tristan Donovan, 2017, 'Ministers Urged to Back Full-Time Youth Volunteering', *CYPN*, 16 November.

[68] Joe Lepper, 2018, '"Government rules out full-time social action role for NCS"', *CYPN*, 25 July.

[69] Derren Hayes, 2018, 'Government-commissioned report recommends paid community work for 100,000 young people', *CYPN*, 24 September.

[70] Danny Kruger, 2020, *Levelling up our communities: proposals for a new social covenant*, September, pp. 28, 33, https://www.dannykruger.org.uk/sites/www.dannykruger.org.uk/files/2020-09/Levelling%20Up%20Our%20Communities-Danny%20Kruger.pdf,    UK Parliament, 2020, 'Levelling Up Our Communities', accessed 29 December 2020, https://www.dannykruger.org.uk/communities-report.

[71] Amrit Virdi, 2023, 'DCMS and NCS Trust to fund UK Year of Service programme', *CYPN*, 2 October.

- How consciously and consistently have the actual practices been developed using open youth work's defining process-led approaches?
- Where have these been used, and how have they contributed to achieving the reported impacts on and benefits for the young people involved?

These questions, however, need to be located with a broader policy issue which remained unresolved throughout this period: the government's reluctance to, as a minimum, commit explicitly to reinstating all the open access facilities which had been closed after 2010, including providing the necessary resources for their staffing and everyday running costs. Though, as outlined in the last chapter, some limited funding was provided particularly through the YIF, huge gaps remained (and remain). This was especially true of spaces (including for detached work) to which young people could just turn up with their mates and then choose whether (or not) to take part in a volunteering or indeed a curriculum-defined or 'youth voice' activity.

Rather than prioritising the restoration of these kinds of lost facilities, the government's attention (and money) in this period was focused much more on broadening the conception of 'youth work' in order to justify locating youth workers in organisations and schemes whose aims and ways of working were often very different. This development is explored in more detail in the next chapter.

# CHAPTER 5

# Redefining and Repurposing Youth Work

**Abstract** Over the period covered by this book, policy-makers and practitioners broadened the concept of 'youth work' to include the practices of organisations and projects, often state-funded, which targeted young people's anti-social behaviour, their school attendance, employment prospects and mental health. With some of these *requiring* young people's participation, their starting points and approaches could be very different from—indeed sometimes at variance with—some of open youth work's key defining features. The endorsement of these wider conceptions of youth work by policy-makers, academics and some within the youth sector itself can be seen as helping to divert attention and resources from open youth work provision and its distinctive ways of working with young people.

**Keywords** Targeted 'youth work' • Anti-social behaviour • School attendance • Employment • Mental health • Resourcing open youth work

## REDEFINING 'YOUTH WORK'

Throughout this period, local and national policy-makers saw youth workers as important, even crucial, for responding to a range of high-priority 'youth problems'—a position which attracted a number of endorsements from the NYA:

© The Author(s), under exclusive license to Springer Nature                69
Switzerland AG 2024
B. Davies, *Youth Work Policies in England 2019–2023*,
https://doi.org/10.1007/978-3-031-65636-1_5

- In an interview in 2017, its Chief Executive Leigh Middleton, while acknowledging that youth work 'could be healthier', rejected the view that it was 'in total crisis' on the grounds that 'many youth workers (are) employed today … in schools, children's services, troubled families and early help and prevention'.[1]
- Two years later, NYA based its 'Update' on the routes to validated youth work qualifications on the premise that 'youth work and its methods are … well recognised and supported across a wide range of applications'.[2]
- Its paper *Youth Work in England* noted that 'local authorities … utilise youth work for different purposes'.[3]
- By January 2023, the Level 4 Certificate in Professional Development (Youth Work) was in part aimed at those 'who wish to make use of Youth Work methods in the services they offer, such as social workers, police officers, those working in the emergency services and teachers'.[4]
- In a report published in November 2023 on 'the social cost of youth work cuts', sub-titled 'Preventing youth offending through youth work', NYA made the case 'for greater collaboration between youth work and youth justice settings'.[5]

Others in and around the youth work sector also argued for 'youth work' to be used preventatively and/or remedially in a wide range of settings.

[1] Neil Puffett, 2017, 'Steering youth work's future: Leigh Middleton, managing director, National Youth Agency', *CYPN*, 26 September

[2] NYA, 2019, 'An Update of Routes into Youth Work', 30 July, https://www.nya.org.uk/an-update-on-routes-into-youth-work/

[3] NYA, 2023, *Youth Work in England: Policy, Practice and the National Occupational Standards,* ?April, p4, https://nya.org.uk/wp-content/uploads/2024/02/NOS-Document-102023-1.pdf.

[4] NYA, 2023, 'New qualification for youth work professionals to build skills of sector', 12 January, https://www.nya.org.uk/new-qualification-for-youth-work-professionals-to-build-skills-of-sector/#:~:text=Safeguarding%20Hub-,New%20qualification%20for%20youth%20work%20professionals%20to%20build%20skills%20of,their%20skills%20in%20specialist%20areas.

[5] NYA, 2023, *The social cost of youth work cuts: Preventing youth offending through youth work,* November, https://s3.eu-west-1.amazonaws.com/assets.nya2.joltrouter.net/wp-content/uploads/2023/11/02113902/NYA-Report-The-social-cost-of-youth-work-cuts-%E2%80%93-Preventing-youth-offending-through-youth-work.pdf.

- In a paper published just before the 2019 general election committing it to a full reinstatement of the lost open youth work facilities, the Labour Party made repeated references to the role of trained youth workers in dealing with young people's anti-social behaviour, in skilling and equipping them to 'learn and earn' and in supporting their 'health and wellbeing'.[6] At its annual conference four years later, it added detail to this by promising if elected to launch a 'Sure Start for teenagers' comprising 90 'youth hubs' across the country. Part of a ten-year cross-government 'tough love' programme, this would be designed to tackle knife crime and poor mental health by bringing together youth workers, mental health specialists and neighbourhood police officers.[7]
- In October 2020, a pilot training programme at Feltham Young Offenders Institution—judged a 'great success'—provided over 3000 youth work sessions to develop prison officers' 'youth work skills' to Youth Work Qualification Level 2.[8]
- At an NYA-organised 'youth work summit' in November 2021, the Chair of the Youth Justice Board described youth workers as '… an important part of the (diversion) picture (because) they are often the bridge between children and statutory services'.[9]
- The following February, Paul Oginsky, then Chief Executive of a 'youth mutual' working across Lancashire and Cheshire and a former adviser to Prime Minister David Cameron, pressed for young people to have greater access to youth services as a way of helping to 'reduce conflict and violence'.[10]
- In November 2023, the Mayor of London, Sadiq Khan, allocated £160,000 to launch Trust Youth Allies, a pilot project for training youth workers to support young victims of often unreported crimes.

[6] Labour Party, 2019, *Only Young Once: The Labour Party's Vision for Rebuilding Youth Services*, p. 10, October.

[7] Fiona Simpson, 2023, 'Labour Conference 2023: Yvette Cooper reveals "Sure Start for teenagers" plan', *CYPN*, 10 October; Rajeev Syal and Pippa Crerar, 2023, 'Labour will set up "young futures" youth programme to tackle knife crime', *Guardian*, 9 October.

[8] Fiona Simpson, 2020, 'Youth work training scheme "improved YOI staff's relationships with young people"', *CYPN*, 23 October.

[9] Derren Hayes, 2021, 'Youth work diversion role lauded' *CYPN*, 30 November.

[10] Fiona Simpson, 2022, 'Youth work central to reducing knife crime, say former government adviser', *CYPN*, 24 February.

This was to be delivered in five of the capital's boroughs with 'high youth victimisation and low trust in the police'.[11]

As austerity took its toll and local youth services were closed down, many youth workers anyway found themselves needing to take jobs in organisations—youth offending teams, schools, sports programmes, mental health projects, hospitals and housing associations[12]—whose core purposes, policies, structures and approaches were very different from those of an open youth work facility. Not only here might a young person's participation sometimes be compulsory, but the processes for engaging with them were often shaped more by pre-defined agendas, curricula and programmes than by the workers' exploration of and responses to the personal and shared interests and concerns of the young people who actually participated.

Within these settings, such personally developmental aspirations and potential may still have attracted attention. Sally Carr, the director of StreetGames North West and an NYA trustee, pointed for example to possible long-term physical and mental health gains from 'blending ... the coaching style of sports and the collaborative principles of youth work'. She also highlighted how this approach could help break through some of those embedded structural barriers faced by LGBTQ+ young people and by those from ethnic minorities and 'lower economic groups'.[13]

What nonetheless repeatedly emerged as a (even the) driver for extending youth work's 'reach' into other youth settings was 'preventative targeting'—as when, for example, Carr also pointed to its potential for '... reducing the risk of movement into crime' and 'supporting improvements in children' education'.[14] As, from early 2020, the often-severe Covid impacts on young people became clear, expectations of youth work's potential for delivering this targeted practice grew further.

---

[11] Joe Lepper, 2023, 'Youth workers to be trained to support young victims of unreported crime', *CYPN*, 2 November.

[12] See also NYA, 2019, 'An Update of Routes into Youth Work', 30 July, https://www.nya.org.uk/an-update-on-routes-into-youth-work/.

[13] Sally Carr, 2022, 'Strike the right balance to enhance the youth work offer through sport', *CYPN*, 1 June; See also Amanda Vernalls, 2022, 'Youth work and sport: research evidence', *CYPN*, 1 June.

[14] Sally Carr (2022).

## 'YOUTH VIOLENCE'

One particularly high government priority for such targeting was 'youth violence'—especially knife crime. Even before the pandemic, the Ministry of Justice had been monitoring a Metropolitan Police 'Divert' project in London which, with £300,000 funding from the Home Office, had assigned youth workers to Camden and Islington police stations to support young people and their families caught up in the justice system.[15] The project was later integrated into a wider 'Violence Reduction Unit' (VRU) programme which, using a 'public health' approach to combating knife crime, had first been developed in Glasgow.[16]

By mid-2022, funded by £70 million from the Home Office, 18 VRUs were operating across England.[17] The London Units—later extended by a pilot 'Engage' project[18]—were initially allocated an additional £550,000 from a Lord Mayor's VRU Fund with a brief which included doubling the 'dozens of youth workers' in the capital's police stations. By May 2022, with the London grant by then increased to £3 million, these 'intervention coaches' were said to have 'supported away from violence' more than 300 10–18-year-olds arrested in Camden, Enfield and Redbridge.[19]

Such local 'violence reduction' initiatives were developed further the following August, including by 'youth work services', using a £4.5 million grant from a London Crime Prevention Fund.[20] Nine months later, the London Mayor's Fund allotted an additional £2.1 million for increasing the number of specially trained youth workers based in the Metropolitan

[15] Neil Puffett, 2020, 'Youth workers could be deployed in police stations "to tackle disproportionality"'. *CYPN*, 18 February.

[16] Libby Brooks, 2024, 'How a pioneering Scottish violence reduction unit achieved radical change, 25 February.

[17] Ciaran Thapar, 2021, *Cut Short: Youth Violence, Loss and Hope n the City*, Viking, pp. 180, 287–9; Derren Hayes, 2022, 'Interview: Lib Peck, Director of the Mayor of London's Violence Reduction Unit' *CYPN*, 21 June.

[18] Mayor of London, 2022, 'London's VRU invests £3m to divert more young people from violence', 18 May, https://www.london.gov.uk/press-releases/mayoral/londons-vru-invests-3m-in-young-people.

[19] Derren Hayes, 2020, 'Youth workers to be trained to lead violence response in London', *CYPN*, 8 June; Fiona Simpson, 2022, '£3m fund to place youth workers in more London police stations', *CYPN*, 18 May. See also Jack Rowlands, 2020, How we DIVERT young people away from crime and towards opportunity', 29 April, https://www.london.gov.uk/city-hall-blog/how-we-divert-young-people-away-crime-and-towards-opportunity.

[20] Fiona Simpson, 2022, 'Youth work key to London's £5m violence prevention programme', *CYPN*, 18 August.

Police's 12 basic command units where 'custody suites' had already supported over 1500 10–18-year-olds in trouble with the law.[21] The Fund had also by then provided £7.9 million for three years to embed youth workers in London A&E departments, briefed to help young people injured by violent crime to move away from criminal activity.[22]

Support from government departments as well as from non-statutory bodies enabled similar developments outside London. By early 2020, for example, the Redthread organisation—'mission: to empower young people to thrive ... by integrating trauma-informed youth work into the health sector'—was supporting 14–24-year-olds judged to be at risk of criminal exploitation and gang violence in seven locations including some in the Midlands.[23]

In March 2021, in *Between The Lines*,[24] NYA made the case for a more strategic youth worker role in tackling young people's involvement in 'youth violence' overall and in county lines drug activities specifically. Starting from a recognition of 'a lack of sufficient youth services and support for young people in many county towns and rural areas', it highlighted their need for 'safe spaces in their communities, to gain trust and disclose their problems or ask for help'. With 'meaningful youth engagement ... included as a funding condition for Violence Reduction Units', it proposed that

*Youth services ... (be) embedded in a public health approach for county lines ... which includes building the capacity and up-skilling of youth and community groups, including ... working with young people 'where they're at'.*

The NYA proposals attracted some, at least implicit, wider support. In November 2022, for example, the former children's Commissioner for England, Anne Longfield, recommended the creation by 2027 of an England-wide network of 1000 Sure Start 'community hubs' for

---

[21] Derren Hayes, 2023, 'London Mayor funds more youth workers in custody suites' *CYPN*, 21 April.

[22] Fiona Simpson, 2022, 'Sadiq Khan announces £8m funding to embed youth workers in emergency departments', *CYPN*, 7 October.

[23] Redthread, at https://www.redthread.org.uk/about-us/, accessed 2 April 2023; Neil Puffett, 2020, 'Youth workers could be deployed in police stations "to tackle disproportionality"'., *CYPN*, 18 February.

[24] NYA, 2021, *Between The Lines*, March, https://www.nya.org.uk/resource/between-the-lines/.

teenagers. Their role would be to 'guide, support and inspire' young people vulnerable to exploitation by criminal gangs, including by recruiting
an 'army' of 10,000 additional youth workers to 'link schools and youth
offending services'.[25] This was followed in March 2023 by a government
promise that a network of 'outdoor learning schemes' would be 'one of
the key causes' to be funded out of the £892 million of 'dormant assets'[26]
(see Chap. 3).

Despite the range of funding routes and proposed initiatives, by April
2022, the NAO was predicting that, within two years in England and
Wales, the number of children in custody would double—the result in part
of tougher sentencing regimes following the passing of a police and sentencing bill and of court backlogs caused by Covid delays.[27] Upward
trends of this kind seemed even more likely in the wake of a 'zero-tolerance'
Anti-social Behaviour Action Plan announced by the government in
March 2023. Intended to '… prevent (young people) from offending in
the first place', this also promised 'an extra one million hours of youth
services in areas with the highest rates of anti-social behaviour' whose
over-riding emphasis still was on a further extension of police powers.[28]

A focus on deterring young people's anti-social behaviour was central,
too, to the £3.7 million allocated from the government's Million Hour
Fund in August 2023 so that 420 'youth services across England … in
areas of high need' could stay open longer. As well as offering the young
people sports and arts opportunities, day trips and cooking lessons, these
would also provide them with 'someone to talk to, something to do and
somewhere to go throughout the summer holidays'.[29]

---

[25] Derren Hayes, 2022, 'Longfield Commission sets out "Sure Start for Teenagers" plans',
*CYPN*, 4 November; Fiona Simpson, 2022, 'Sector backs Longfield's call for "Sure Start for
Teenagers"', *CYPN*, 7 November; Derren Hayes, 2022, 'Interview: Anne Longfield on how
Commission sets out action to tackle youth violence', *CYPN* 1 December.

[26] Emily Harle, 2023, 'Outdoor learning schemes to benefit from £892m fund', *CYPN*,
24 March.

[27] Sally Weale, 2022, 'Number of children in England and Wales set to double by 2024',
*Guardian*, 28 April.

[28] GOV.UK, 2023, 'Press release: Action plan to crack down on anti-social behaviour',
26 March, https://www.gov.uk/government/news/action-plan-to-crack-down-on-anti-
social-behaviour.

[29] Clare Herrom, 2023, 'Youth services granted funding to deter anti-social behaviour',
*CYPN*, 31 August.

## SCHOOLING AND JOBS

As the impacts of the pandemic and its lockdowns on young people became clear, ambitious proposals also emerged for increasing youth workers' role in tackling what were seen as two inter-related issues: ensuring young people re-engaged in school and improving their job prospects. These concerns were driven by evidence—for example, in a 2022 Centre for Youth Justice report—that by the 2020 autumn term, 'schools with the most disadvantaged intake (were) 10 times as likely to have a class-worth of severely absent pupils'[30] (see Chap. 2). Six months later, with helping young people recover from the pandemic as one of the concerns, an exchange took place at an MPs' Education Select Committee meeting between its Chair and a sixth form college Principal on youth work's potential for improving educational attainment. This prompted the latter to talk of 'a missed opportunity in secondary schools to utilise youth centres … as part of extended days …'[31]

Here too, in increasingly systematic ways, NYA had by then been addressing these possibilities. As early as June 2020, it had highlighted 'the need to bring formal education (schools and colleges) and non-formal education (youth work and youth services) together'. It had gone on to recommend 'an urgent package of support to deploy youth workers for summer schools, detached/outreach youth work and activities in schools'. It had also proposed a 'Youth Service Guarantee to secure universal access to youth work; as a baseline on which a local youth offer from schools and community-based provision can flourish'. This, the Agency said, would ensure that one of its key demands was met—for two qualified youth workers and a team of youth support workers and trained volunteers in every secondary school catchment area[32] (see Chap. 4).

Expanding on the proposal, the following month, Leigh Middleton talked of 'an unnecessary divide with schools being seen as education and youth work seen largely as leisure'. For reaching 'some of the most

---

[30] Centre for Social Justice, 2022, 'Lost but not forgotten: the reality of severe absence in schools post-lockdown', January, https://www.centreforsocialjustice.org.uk/wp-content/uploads/2022/01/CSJ-Lost_but_not_forgotten-2.pdf.

[31] Fiona Simpson, 2022, 'Schools must link with youth services to boost pupil wellbeing, MPs told', *CYPN*, 9 February.

[32] NYA, 2020, *Time out: Re-imagining schools – a youth work response to Covid-19*, June; Nina Jacobs, 2020, 'Mobilise youth workers to help young people ease out of lockdown, says NYA', *CYPN*, 26 June.

vulnerable', he argued that this gap needed to be bridged as 'youth work has a bigger role to play to ensure no young person is "left behind"'.[33] NYA followed up these proposals in March and April 2022 by announcing a review co-chaired by former Children's Minister Tim Loughton and former shadow education secretary Kate Green.[34] Loughton subsequently outlined its brief as to look at 'collaboration of youth work with schools, for young people to engage in education, learn new skills and improve their life chances'.[35]

The review's 62-page report published in June 2023[36] brought together substantial new evidence, including from young people, acquired via online hearings and from visits to services. Key 'areas for development' identified included 'Education and wellbeing'; 'School absenteeism'; 'Holiday Activities and Food … Programme'; 'Enrichment'—through for example extra-curricular activities; 'Local youth partnerships …'; and 'Ways of working between school and youth organisations'. It also proposed that young people be re-engaged in education through 'outreach care and detached youth work'.

Its 12 recommendations included:

- 'An over-arching cross-department youth policy' with oversight by a Youth Minister at the Department for Education with a remit and authority across departments.
- 'A National Youth Strategy'.
- 'Stable and joined-up funding …'
- 'Integrating youth work values and approaches in initial teacher training …'

[33] NYA, 2020, *A youth work response to Covid-19*, NYA, July, https://www.nya.org.uk/resource/nya-covid-19-response-july-2020/; Leigh Middleton, 2020, 'Expert view: "It's time for schools and youth workers to come together to address the challenges of the past-pandemic world"', *CYPN*, 28 July.

[34] NYA, 2022, 'Review of the role and contribution of Youth Work with Schools'(2022), https://www.nya.org.uk/youth-work-schools-review/; Joe Lepper, 2022, 'NYA launches review of youth workers in schools', *CYPN*, 30 March.

[35] NYA, 2022, 'Call for Evidence: "Opportunities for All – Youth Work and Schools"', 29 March, https://www.nya.org.uk/call-for-evidence-opportunities-for-all-youth-work-and-schools/.

[36] NYA, 2023, *Better Together: Youth work in schools – Complementing formal education to change young people's lives*, June, https://www.nya.org.uk/youth-work-with-schools/; Emily Harle, 2023, 'Youth work in schools key to improving attendance rates, NYA inquiry finds', *CYPN*, 21 June.

- A 'transition route from teaching to youth work'.
- 'An enhanced (OFSTED) inspection framework …'

Co-inciding with the appearance of the NYA report was an announcement by the NCS and the DfE that, in consultation with the DCMS, they had jointly commissioned a new study into the links between schools and local youth work opportunities for young people.[37] To be carried out by UK Youth and the Centre for Education and Youth, its aim was to explore how collaboration and co-ordination between the wider education and youth sectors could be strengthened. Within the broader context of 'education and enrichment' and with the findings aimed at informing national policy, activities such as 'social action', 'outdoor play', and sport and art were to be examined to produce ten case studies illustrating how different approaches to collaboration worked in practice.

This was followed in November by the launch of a £2.7 million pilot scheme funded by the DCMS and the DfE as part of the government's Levelling Up agenda. Working with local businesses, charities, multi-academy trusts (see Chap. 2) and local councils, this was to provide 'enrichment activities' in 200 secondary schools in the North East, North West and East of England.[38]

Reflecting often deeply embedded wider expectations of what schooling could and should be doing, youth work was also seen as potentially valuable in helping to prepare young people for the labour market and improving their employment opportunities. With these further diminished by the pandemic, five national organisations including the Prince's Trust published a report in July 2021 sub-titled 'Building an Opportunity Guarantee' which also rode on the back of the government's 'levelling up' rhetoric.[39] This was underpinned by substantial evidence of how 'young people have been hit worst by the labour market crisis'—exemplified by

[37] Baz Ramaiah, 2023, 'NCS Trust and The Duke of Edinburgh's Award partner with The Centre for Education and Youth and UK Youth to carry out new research on education and enrichment', Centre for Education and Youth, 22 June, https://cfey.org/news-and-events/2023/06/ncs-trust-and-the-duke-of-edinburghs-award-partner-with-the-centre-for-education-and-youth-and-uk-youth-to-carry-out-new-research-on-education-and-enrichment/; Fiona Simpson, 2023, 'Major study to examine youth sector collaboration with schools', *CYPN*, 26 June.

[38] Joe Lepper, 2023, 'National Citizens Service partners with DoE for school activities', *CYPN*, 1 November.

[39] Josh Adcock, 2021, *Levelling up for young people: Building an Opportunity Guarantee*, Institute for Employment Studies/Impetus/Princes Trust/Youth Employment UK/youth Futures Foundation, July, https://www.youthemployment.org.uk/dev/wp-content/themes/yeuk/files/opportunity-guarantee-tw.pdf.

'the decline in working hours for young people with no qualifications (34%) … (being) five times higher during the Covid crisis than for those with degree-level qualifications (7%)'. The consortium which produced the report sought to ensure that, with young men and Black and Asian people most at risk, 'the age groups who have been most affected …. do not fall behind …' Though never naming youth work or youth workers specifically, the report repeatedly advocated for a 'continuing roll out (of) "Youth Hubs" in partnership with local authorities, employers and the youth employment sector'.

Given schools' often deeply embedded negative view of 'difficult pupils',[40] actually implementing such proposals could pose significant challenges. This was brought into sharp focus in 2022 by the experience of 'Child Q'—a 16-year-old young women falsely accused of carrying drugs who, while she was having a period, was strip-searched by police in her school without a parent, teacher or other 'appropriate person' present to support her.[41]

## MENTAL HEALTH

As illustrated by the £45 million Young London Mayor's Fund mental health allocation in February 2020 to train youth workers and others in 'first aid' mental health,[42] even before the pandemic youth workers were also seen as able to make valuable—even distinctive—responses to young people's growing mental health problems (see Chap. 2). As the impacts on them of Covid and its lockdowns became clear—and as evidence emerged of youth workers' widespread and growing concerns about these[43]—this focus sharpened significantly within the youth work field itself and more widely.

In early 2022, for example, UK Youth collaborated with the Thriving Minds Foundation and the Julia and Hans Rausing Trust to launch a £10 million fund to support young people struggling with mental health

---

[40] See, for example, Ciaran Thapar, 2021, *Cut Short: Youth Violence, Loss and Hope n the City*, Viking, Sections 3 and 5.

[41] Fiona Simpson, 2022, 'Strip-searched by police', *CYPN*, 21 March.

[42] Nina Jacobs, 2020, 'Mental health first aid training to expand to youth clubs', *CYPN*, 7 February.

[43] Barnarado's/King's College London, 2022, 'Practitioners' concerns for issues facing young people', 1 June, https://www.barnardos.org.uk/research/practitioners-concerns-issues-facing-young-people.

issues.[44] By the end of May, its Chief Executive was reporting that 'the demand has totally outstripped our funding' as, within three weeks of the Fund's opening, applications had been received from 1000 organisations totalling £30 million a year. She also highlighted that '… youth workers can spot the signs that a young person is experiencing difficulties and can support them to open up, talk through what they are going through and seek help if they need it'.[45]

With this as a main rationale, in August 2022, a Back Youth Alliance initiative supported by amongst others, the YMCA, the Scouts, UK Youth, BYC, OnSide and the NYA called on the government to set up a £300 million Youth Potential Fund with the overall purpose, noted earlier, of training an additional 10,000 qualified youth workers and 30,000 volunteers. Drawing again on money from the Dormant Assets Scheme with, the government said, £880 million added, the Fund's aims included increasing young people's access 'to local clubs and activities that improve (their) confidence, self–esteem, skills and ability to make friends' and to 'trained and supported trusted adults (including volunteers) to give (them) someone to talk to'.[46]

These possibilities were explored in a grounded way by a pilot project which placed two psychologists in the Haringey Bruce Grove Youth Cub in London to train and advise its workers on 'wellbeing issues'. In September 2022, a Centre for Mental Health evaluation of the scheme concluded that placing mental health workers in a youth club 'takes the stigma away from mental health' and so 'enabl(es) them to reach young people who would not normally trust mental health services'.[47]

[44] Fiona Simpson, 2022, 'UK Youth launches £10M mental health fund', *CYPN*, 28 February. See also for example Andie Reynolds and Alison Ni Charraighe, 2022, 'Post-Covid Youth Work and Mental Wellbeing of Young People Across Scotland and England', *Concept*, Vol 13, No 2, Summer.

[45] Fiona Simpson, 2022, 'UK Youth fund receives 1,000 applications in three weeks' *CYPN*, 27 May.

[46] Scouts, 2022, 'Back Youth Alliance calls for investment in young people's mental health and wellbeing', 19 August, https://www.scouts.org.uk/news/2022/august/back-youth-alliance/; Joe Lepper, 2022, 'Youth charities make case for £300M mental health fund' *CYPN*, 25 August.

[47] Androulla Harris, Huong Le, Zoë McHayle and Yasmin Ahmadzadeh, 2022, *Always there for us: Evaluating Project Future's work at Bruce Grove youth club*, Centre for Mental Health, 21 September, https://www.centreformentalhealth.org.uk/publications/always-there-us; Joe Lepper, 2022, 'Youth club psychologist pilot prompts call for more mental health partnerships'. *CYPN*, 21 September.

These conclusions were given added weight by evidence from two separate studies published in April and May 2022. One revealed that many young people from 'racialised communities' 'do not trust mental health services' because—in contrast to how an open youth work project might be committed to respond—they experienced 'higher levels of stigma and ... greater risk of coercion'.[48] The second study highlighted youth workers' need for just the kinds of additional inputs—and resources—provided by the Bruce Grove project. Though 87 per cent of its respondents reported that they were frequently offering young people mental health support, many said they weren't always confident that they were spotting the warning signs of distress while, for signposting young people for additional help, only just over half felt supported by mental health specialists.[49]

## Possible Impacts on Open Youth Work?

During 2022–23, some local councils made small increases in their spending on open youth work, with the number of youth centres increasing for the first time in over a decade from 398 in 2021/22 to 427 in 2022/23.[50] However, the developments outlined in this chapter, which assumed that trained youth workers would be used increasingly to respond preventively and remedially to young people's problems,[51] were often resourced by a government which was continuing to cut its Rate Support Grant and other financial support for local authorities (see Chap. 3).

Though hard evidence is not available, this widening of the conception of 'youth work' therefore prompts at least two exploratory questions.

[48] Joe Lepper, 2022, 'Mental health call to reform youth support in racialised communities', *CYPN*, 27 April.

[49] Fiona Simpson, 2022, 'Youth workers "poorly equipped" to provide mental health support, research finds'. *CYPN*, 21 April.

[50] Derren Hayes, 2024, 'English councils increase spending on youth services', *CYPN*, 31 February.

[51] See, for example, NYA, 2020, *Out of Sight: Vulnerable Young People: COVID-19 Response*, April, https://www.nya.org.uk/resource/out-of-sight-vulnerable-young-people-covid-19-response/; Janet Batsleer et al. 2021, 'The Importance of Our Wild Stories: The Citizens Enquiry into Youth Work in the Time of Covid-19', *Youth and Policy*, 18 January; Tracie Trimmer-Platman, 2022, 'Embrace unashamedly the therapeutic qualities and benefits of youth work to young people and communities', *Research in Teacher Education*, Vol 12, No 1, May, pp. 20–23; Sally Carr, 2022, 'And Someone to Talk To: The role of Therapeutic Youth Work, *Youth and Policy*, 6 November.

Firstly, to what extent, albeit indirectly, did it shift attention and resources away from open youth work and in particular from a government commitment to fully reinstate those lost 'spaces' which, pre-austerity, significant numbers of young people were choosing as a potentially personally supportive educational facility outside school?

And secondly, why at the local level would a council risk allocating its already severely restricted resources to, say, a small youth club focused on what *these* young people say they want from it, when government money was on offer to embed its youth workers in programmes which define their expected 'outcomes' in advance and may even require attendance?

# CHAPTER 6

# The Voluntary Sector: The 'Traditional'— And the New

**Abstract** The government's declared 'vision' for the voluntary youth sector was to locate it within its August 2018 civil society policy strategy. Though this was not fully realised, two relatively new youth-focused programmes—the National Citizens Service and OnSide—did attract significant state funding. However, the former was still available only to 16- and 17-year-olds, while the latter posed some significant questions from an open youth work perspective. One, for example, was how far its Youth Zones across the country were delivering open youth work to their 'thousands' of users; another was whether small neighbourhood-based facilities focused on this practice would be able to compete for the still limited state resources available with high profile online funding bids promising large state-of-the-art buildings.

**Keywords** State funding • Civil society strategy • National Citizens Service • OnSide Youth Zones • Resourcing open youth work

## THE WIDER 'CIVIL SOCIETY' STRATEGY

Throughout this period, the government claimed that it saw the voluntary youth sector as operating within its wider 'civil society' strategy—published in August 2018 and shaped in part by a neo-liberal concern to

B. Davies, *Youth Work Policies in England 2019–2023*,
https://doi.org/10.1007/978-3-031-65636-1_6

reduce the role of the state.[1] In a statement posted on the DCMS website in October 2019,[2] Baroness Barran, then Under-Secretary of State for Civil Society, reflected on some of the strategy's more immediate aspirations. She, for example, talked of 'reaffirming the ties that bind us together' and of a '… ten-year vision for how government can work with and support civil society to improve lives and create a fairer society for all'. Through what she labelled 'social value', she claimed that the government could also

> … help to bring focus, unlock potential, and—where possible—convene, catalyse and fund activity to support people within communities who, together, can make a real difference.

She then listed a range of what she saw as relevant youth-focused initiatives:

- The NCS, which in the previous year had attracted 100,000 young people.
- An 'investment' of £5 million 'to create over 10,000 new places in unformed youth groups such as Fire Cadets and Scouts for young people in disadvantaged areas'.
- The allocation of £40 million to the #iwill Fund for young people's 'volunteering and community engagement'; and the creation of 'three (new) youth voice pilot projects' (see Chap. 4).
- Funding for new routes to youth work qualifications (see Chap. 8).
- A dormant bank accounts allocation of £90 million 'to support the most disadvantaged young people into meaningful employment'.

As one of the strategy's 'next steps', she pointed to the '£500 million Youth Investment Fund' which the Chancellor had announced the previous month as part of a government 'Youth Offer' (see Chap. 3). This was followed in June 2022 by invitations to organisations to apply for £250,000 grants from a Local Capacity Building Fund set up to support 8–10 local youth partnerships in areas that qualified for YIF money. The partnerships

---

[1] GOV.UK, 2018, *Civil Society Strategy: building a future that works for everyone*, 9 August, https://www.gov.uk/government/publications/civil-society-strategy-building-a-future-that-works-for-everyone.

[2] DCMS, 2019, '1.#OurCivilSociety – Reflections from Baroness Barron', 25 October, https://www.gov.uk/government/publications/our-civil-society/ourcivilsociety.

had to include 'statutory and civil society members ... involved in the delivery, commissioning or planning (of) services for young people' with the objective of 'boost(ing) the range, quality and sustainability of front-line services for young people through greater coordination and cooperation'.[3]

Evidence over the period, however, suggested that the government often struggled to realise this 'vision'.

- An NYA paper published in July 2019 indicated that, despite an increasing reliance on volunteer workers, 'they suffer from (having) little recognised available training or on the job support'.[4]
- In its 'manifesto' released in the run-up to the December 2019 General Election, the National Council for Voluntary Organisations (NCVO) pressed the new government to do more to engage with civil society, not least by increasing funding for charities, deprived communities and local councils. It also urged that, post-Brexit, the lost EU funding be replaced at 'a comparable level'.[5]
- After the election—together with some more optimistic messages—NCVO spelt out a voluntary sector perspective on issues which, again especially post-Brexit, were still 'in urgent need of being properly addressed'. These included 'education and local government, a green industrial revolution, and health and social care'.[6]
- In January 2020, a report from the think tank New Philanthropy Capital revealed a north-south divide in charitable provision, with the availability of volunteers and the levels of philanthropic donations and council grants disproportionately concentrated in England's most affluent areas.[7]

---

[3] GOV.UK, 2022, 'Guidance – Applying to the local Capacity Building Fund for local youth partnerships', 31 May, https://www.gov.uk/guidance/applying-to-the-local-capacity-building-fund-for-local-youth-partnerships.

[4] NYA, 2019, 'An Update on Routes into Youth Work', 30 July, https://www.nya.org.uk/an-update-on-roures-into-youth-work.

[5] Liam Kay, 2019, 'NCVO calls on the next government to do more to engage with civil society', *Third Sector*, 12 November.

[6] Michael Birtwistle etc., 2020, *The Road Ahead: A Review of the Voluntary Sector's Operating Environment*, NCVO, January, downloadable via https://www.basw.co.uk/resources/road-ahead-review-voluntary-sector%E2%80%99s-operating-environment.

[7] Patrick Butler, 2020, 'Charities crowded in affluent areas instead of where they are needed, say thinktank', *Guardian*, 17 January.

- A number of voluntary organisations—including the Charity Aid Foundation and NCVO—responded angrily to the assertion in November 2020 by the then-chair of the Charity Commission, Baroness Tina Stowell, that 'if you want to improve lives and strengthen communities through charity, you need to leave party politics and the culture wars out of it'.[8]
- The following month, a report from the Law Family Commission on Civil Society talked of the sector being 'undervalued and overlooked' in national decision-making and of a 'collective failure to properly value what civil society delivers'.[9] The culture secretary Oliver Dowden, though pointing to the government's '£750m investment in the sector when the Covid-19 crisis hit', also acknowledged that the pandemic had revealed that Whitehall didn't know as much about civil society as it thought it did.[10]
- Faced with an estimated shortfall in income as a result of the Covid crisis, in February 2021, hundreds of the UK's biggest charities including Comic Relief and the Samaritans sent a joint letter to Prime Minister Boris Johnson calling for a government emergency support fund for the voluntary sector.[11]
- A month later, the Association of Chief Executives of Voluntary Organisations stated publicly that, as the Spring budget hadn't offered any support specifically for charities, the government had 'once again failed to recognise the vital role civil society plays' and accused it of 'taking the charity sector for granted'.[12]
- Albeit less explicitly, reservations about the government's treatment of the sector seemed to be reflected, too, in a Parliamentary select committee conclusion—rejected by the DCMS—that the short-listing for a new Chair of the Charity Commission in 2022 had

---

[8] Stephen Delahunty, 2020, 'Fury as commission chair says charities should not be involved "party politics and culture wars"', *Third Sector*, 30 November.

[9] Commission on Civil Action, 2020, *Civil Action: Exploring the civil society's potential in the 2020s*, December, p. 9, https://civilsocietycommission.org/wp-content/uploads/2021/01/Law-Family-Commission-on-Civil-Society_Civil-Action.pdf.

[10] Stephen Delahunty, 2020, 'We want to unleash the power of civil society, culture secretary says', *Third Sector*, 1 December.

[11] Patrick Butler, 2021, 'UK charities urgently call on PM to set up emergency fund' *Guardian*, 17 February.

[12] Andy Rickets, 2021, 'Budget reaction: Charity sector being "taken for granted" by government', *Third Sector*, 3 March.

lacked diversity and had resulted in a 'slapdash and unimaginative' choice.[13]

All this, moreover, was happening at a time when, as they struggled to avoid bankruptcy, many local councils were making cuts to their funding for local charities which, for some, was putting their survival at risk (see Chap. 3).

By mid-2023, the best response the government seemed able to make to these limitations and constraints was a 'promise' by the charities minister Stuart Andrews that it would make money available to charities 'as soon as we can'.[14]

## THE 'TRADITIONAL' VOLUNTARY YOUTH SECTOR ...

### Developing the Practice

It was within these broader policy and funding contexts that voluntary youth organisations—some with histories going back decades—sought to develop their practice for responding to the growing pressures facing both young people and the sector itself.

After taking on the role played by the National Council for Voluntary Youth Services (NCVYS) until it closed in 2016, UK Youth was particularly proactive on these issues. In an interview in 2020, a year after she became its Chief Executive, Ndidi Okezie described the organisation as 'uniquely placed to play a leading role in terms of strategic investment in the youth sector'. She talked, too, of 'work(ing) with other infrastructure bodies across the voluntary sector and public services'.[15]

Nine months later, explaining UK Youth as 'an open network of over 8000 youth organisations and national partners ... focused on unlocking

---

[13] Patrick Butler, 2022, 'MPs reject government's "unimaginative" choice for Charity Commission chair', *Guardian*, 31 March.

[14] Andy Ryke, 2023, 'Charities minister promises to deliver £100m of emergency funds "as soon as we can"', *Third Sector*, accessed 16 June, https://www.thirdsector.co.uk/charities-minister-promises-deliver-100m-emergency-funds-as-soon-can/policy-and-politics/articl e/1826342?bulletin=thirdsectorweekly&utm_medium=EMAIL&utm_ campaign=eNews%20Bulletin&utm_source=20230616&utm_content=Third%20 Sector%20Weekly%20(19)::&email_hash=.

[15] Derren Hayes, 2020, 'Derren Hayes speaks to the UK Youth chief executive', *CYPN*, 27 October.

youth work as the catalyst of change', Okezie proposed the development of 'a cross-sector strategy across youth services' which by 2025 'champions and delivers effective youth work for all'.[16] One example of how the organisation sought to implement these aspirations was in a 'position statement' on the cost-of-living crisis, published in July 2022. As well as reiterating the need for a 'cross-sector approach', this issued 'calls for action' to 'provide more young people with access to youth workers and trusted adults' and to 'co-design … solutions with young people'.[17]

The responses of UK Youth and other organisations within the youth work sector, separately and collectively, did also sometimes give at least implicit recognition to how many of young people's problems were embedded in underlying structural inequalities.

- In her 2020 interview, Okezie talked of 'respond(ing) with things like the Young & Black campaign' and also (somewhat ambitiously?) of how 'the Black Lives Matter movement really speaks to what youth work does'.
- In April 2021, BYC publicly distanced itself from a controversial government report which had played down the UK's 'race and ethnic disparities'.[18] By late 2022, it was also posting website links to campaigns focused on climate change and votes at 16.[19]
- Prompted by its own research findings—and in the context of what the co-founder of the website 'lastminute.com' identified as a lack of gender diversity in the UK technology industry[20]—in April 2022, Girlguiding introduced courses for Brownies and Guides aimed at challenging girls' assumptions that careers in science, technology

[16] UK Youth, 2021, *Unlocking Youth Work: The catalyst for change that a commitment to young people calls for – Our >>>2025 Strategy*, June, access via https://www.ukyouth.org/2021/06/uk-youth-launches-unlocking-youth-work-2025-strategy/; Joe Lepper, 2021, 'Cross-sector partnership championing youth work to be set up', *CYPN*, 9 June.

[17] UK Youth, 2022, 'UK Youth's position statement on the Cost of Living crisis, 6 July, https://www.ukyouth.org/2022/07/uk-youths-position-statement-on-the-cost-of-living-crisis/.

[18] GOV.UK, 2021, *The report of the Commission on Race and Ethnic Disparities*, 30 March, https://www.gov.uk/government/publications/the-report-of-the-commission-on-race-and-ethnic-disparities; Fiona Simpson, 2021, 'Youth work organisations credited in race report step away from findings', *CYPN*, 13 April.

[19] See https://www.byc.org.uk/campaigns, accessed 12 December 2022.

[20] Jasper Jolly, 2022, 'Gender diversity in UK tech industry 'still terrible', says Martha Lane Fox, *Guardian*, 20 November.

and mathematics were only for boys.[21] It also welcomed transgender girls and non-binary young people into membership, leading to press accusations that it was abandoning its more traditional activities and becoming a campaigning organisation.[22]

For the most part, however, the on-the-ground initiatives of these and other organisations focused mainly on developing young people's individual and peer group knowledge and skills. For example:

- Cross-sector organisations operating through a 'Challenge Group' chaired by Okezie recommended in October 2020 that, to improve what was called their 'urgent financial wellbeing', the two million 16–24-year-olds affected by the Covid pandemic be offered 'meaningful financial education'.[23] This was followed nine months later by a report that a London-based Cubs group was trialling a new 'money skills activity badge' designed to help 6–10-year-olds deal with increasingly 'invisible' financial transactions.[24]
- In September 2021, UK Youth launched a project for 16–25-year-olds from 'racialised communities' aimed at providing them with 'the opportunity to change mental health support for the better and affect real change'.[25]
- In the same month, the Scouts initiated a Squirrels programme for four- and five-year-olds, focused on supporting 200 'deprived' areas

---

[21] Robert Booth, 2022, 'Brownies to learn coding in bid to involve more girls in technology', *Guardian*, 28 April; Fiona Simpson, 2022, 'Girlguiding UK launches programme to teach girls how to code', *CYPN*, 29 April.

[22] Emine Sinmaz, 2023, 'Labour peer Jan Royall: "Girlguiding taught me girls can do anything"', *Guardian*, 26 May.

[23] Fiona Simpson, 2020, 'Youth work leaders back calls for financial training for young people', *CYPN*, 16 October.

[24] Hilary Osborne, 2021, 'Savings to bitcoin: cubs and beavers to launch badge for money skills', *Guardian*, 16 June.

[25] UK Youth, 2021, *Young people from racialised communities re-imaging mental health support*, 2 September, https://www.ukyouth.org/2021/09/young-people-from-racialised-communities-re-imagining-mental-health-support/; Fiona Simpson, 2021, 'UK Youth launches project to shape mental health support for young black people', *CYPN*, 3 September.

across the UK worst affected by Covid-19—particularly Black, Asian and minority ethnic communities.[26]

- Linked to an International Day for the Elimination of Violence Against Women, in November 2022, the young Girlguiders' Advocate Panel wrote to the Education Secretary urging her to improve the teaching of relationships and sex education in schools. Their letter quoted Girlguiding research showing that, even though it was a mandatory part of the curriculum, only 36 per cent of 11–17-year-olds had learned at school about sexual consent.[27]

## Pandemic Impacts—On Practice …

As young people experienced the full impacts of Covid-19 and its lock-downs, youth organisations quickly recognised that if they were to keep their members involved they would often need to engage with them 'remotely' or by using 'outdoor activity and detached work'.[28] In November 2020, for example, the DoE Scheme had endorsed the need for these approaches by funding online training for up to 3500 youth workers.[29] Earlier that year, in March, Girlguiding had launched a two-part 'Adventures at Home' programme offering a daily shared activity on Twitter (now X) and Facebook and weekly resources for participation in online activities.[30] These initiatives prompted it two years later to redraft its online safety policies and help local groups deliver education sessions on digital safeguarding.[31]

[26] Joe Lepper, 2021, Scouts roll out Squirrels programme for pre-school children', *CYPN*, 9 September.

[27] Emily Harle, 2022, 'Girlguiding demands government improves quality of RSE', *CYPN*, 23 November.

[28] UK Youth, 2021, *The Impact of Covid-19 on England's Youth Organisations: Executive Summary*, March, https://www.ukyouth.org/wp-content/uploads/2021/02/UK-Youth-Fund-Report-Executive-Summary_1.pdf.

[29] Joe Lepper, 2020, 'Duke of Edinburgh's Award launches Covid-19 resilience fund', *CYPN*, 25 November.

[30] Fiona Simpson, 2020, 'Coronavirus: uniformed youth groups launch online resources' *CYPN*, 27 March.

[31] Neil Puffett, 2023, Girlguiding UK ensures online safety is at the heart of safeguarding policy and practice', *CYPN*, 3 January.

## ... And on Organisations

A detailed report offering a 'snapshot ... (of) the impact of Covid-19 on the wider youth sector', published by UK Youth in March 2021,[32] drew on over 1750 questionnaire responses from organisations mainly with incomes under £250,000. Even though many young people were by then experiencing 'a variety of barriers to accessing available provision', 66 per cent of the survey respondents said they were facing increased demand—described by 32 per cent as 'significant'. This however was happening at the time when 58 per cent of the organisations were operating at a reduced level, 20 per cent were temporarily closed and pandemic restrictions and its wider financial implications had anyway forced many to reduce their services. (A May 2023 UK Youth report recorded similar findings[33] even though by then the government and much of the media were in effect treating the pandemic as over.)

As the 2021 UK Youth enquiry also revealed, adapting their practice methods to the demands of the Covid crisis was for 57 per cent of respondents also bringing extra, for some unsustainable, staffing and others costs, forcing 62 per cent to spend some or all of their reserves. Despite a predicted increase of 3 per cent in the sector's overall income in the following financial year, this still indicated a total drop of over £14 million compared to the year before Covid arrived. As a result, 44 per cent of organisations were forecasting an income-to-expenditure shortfall and, for 64 per cent, a risk of closing within 12 months—all resulting, the report concluded, in 'a huge gap between the needs of young people and the youth sector's capacity to meet them'.

Based on its findings, the UK Youth report made three main recommendations:

- That long-term funding be made available 'to cover the ongoing core and operational costs of the youth sector'.
- That the sector get financial support to rebuild its workforce.
- That financial support also be provided for organisations to adapt their services. This would include 'investing' in their digital infrastructure 'so that (they) can continue to serve young people when

[32] UK Youth, 2021, *The Impact of Covid-19 on England's Youth Organisations: Executive Summary*, March.
[33] Joe Lepper, 2023, 'Actor highlights "devastating" impact of youth services cuts', *CYPN*, 11 May.

face-to-face provision is not possible'; ensuring that their spaces are Covid-secure; and 'utiliz(ing) methods ... such as detached and mobile youth work'.

The report also proposed more 'non-financial support' through what it called a 'funder-plus model'. This, it said, would enable partnership-working, provide equipment and resources and encourage 'volunteered time across a range of skills to account for a reduced workforce'.

By then, increasing grounded evidence was emerging of why this support was needed. Even though it had created Covid-secure outdoor space for its activities, UK Youth itself was by October 2020 having to cut 14 posts at its Avon Tyrrell residential centre—used the previous year by 71,000 young people—while across the organisation as a whole 65 per cent of staff had been furloughed.[34]

Similar financial pressures were forcing the Scout Association to consider closing at least 500 (7 per cent) of its 7300 groups—prompting one of the many calls at the time for the government to prioritise the release of the YIF money promised a year earlier.[35] With the aim of raising £300,000, one of the Scouts' own responses was to set up a '#RaceAroundtheWorld' challenge to members to get sponsorship for becoming the first of four teams to complete 43,000 miles—equivalent to around the world—by travelling at least a mile a day. Using the government's Kickstart programme for unemployed young people, the Association also planned to create 66 'development officer' posts for young adults[36] and, in collaboration with Girlguiding, to use a £2 million Pears Foundation grant to recruit 5000 new volunteers to fill gaps left by the 15,000 who had left since the pandemic began.[37]

By May 2023, the DoE Scheme was reporting that nearly 538,000 young people were working on getting their award—up by 10 per cent on

---

[34] Fiona Simpson, 2020, 'UK Youth announces job cuts at Avon Tyrrell', *CYPN*, 21 October; Darren Hayes, 2020, 'Interview - Ndidi Okezie, Chief Executive, UK Youth', *CYPN*, 27 October.

[35] Fiona Simpson, 2020, 'More than 500 Scout troops face closure due to Covid-19 pandemic', *CYPN*, 30 October.

[36] Joe Lepper, 2021, 'Scouts launch recruitment campaign to tackle volunteer exodus', *CYPN*, 26 May.

[37] Neil Puffett, 2021, 'Scouts and Girlguiding join forces to recruit volunteers', *CYPN*, 10 May.

the previous year and the highest number ever recruited.[38] In June, both the Scouts and Girlguiding had started to rebuild their membership—the former from 363,000 to 422,000 and the latter by 20 per cent.[39] Despite this progress, Girlguiding announced in mid-2023 that it was still planning to close five of its UK activity centres which by then were being used by less than 10 per cent of its membership and so were no longer financially sustainable.[40] This led to the postponement of a major international event at one of the centres—and to a members' campaign against the closures. By June 2023, this had attracted 31,000 signatures on a petition calling for the decision to be reconsidered, backed by an overnight vigil and a leaders' demonstration outside the Girlguiding London headquarters.[41] A petition initiated by survivors of abuse while they were members was also circulating, calling on the Scout Association to reform its safeguarding procedures to better monitor 'the conduct of volunteers'.[42]

For the government, these more structured models of open youth work nonetheless remained a high priority, including as part of its YIF promise 'to build or refurbish up to 300 youth facilities over the next 3 years'.[43] This included £1.5 million funding to improve the reach of the Scouts, Girlguiding and the St John's Ambulance into 'disadvantaged' areas,[44]

[38] Joe Lepper, 2023, 'Record number of young people taking part in Duke of Edinburgh Award', 10 May.

[39] Robert Booth, 2022, 'Brownies to learn coding in bid to involve more girls in technology' *Guardian*, 28 April; Nicole Weinstein, 2022, 'Girlguiding UK sees spike in new members', *CYPN*, 1 June.

[40] Emily Harle, 2023, 'Girlguiding to close five "financially unsustainable" activity centres', *CYPN*, 22 May.

[41] Emily Harle, 2023, 'Girlguiding urged to reverse activity centre closures', *CYPN*, 7 June; Fiona Simpson, 2023, 'Girlguiding members protest closure of activity centres and overseas units', *CYPN*, 19 June.

[42] Joe Lepper, 2023, 'Abuse survivors call on Scouts to improve safeguarding procedures', *CYPN*, 14 June.

[43] GOV.UK, 2022, 'Press release: £368 million fund to improve youth services in underserved areas open for bids', 1 August, https://www.gov.uk/government/news/368-million-fund-to-improve-youth-services-in-underserved-areas-opens-for-bids?utm_medium=email&utm_campaign=govuk-notifications-topic&utm_source=5810cbc6-db3b-43f8-a5d0-dd55e78b15f6&utm_content=weekly; Youth Investment Fund, 2022, 'About: What is the Youth Investment Fund?', 1 August, https://youthinvestmentfund.org.uk/about/; Joe Lepper, 2022, 'Government invites bids for share of £368m youth services fund', *CYPN*, 3 August.

[44] Joe Lepper, 2022, 'Uniformed youth groups offered £1.5m to expand into disadvantaged areas', *CYPN*, 8 September.

£1.1 million to 'boost' school-based cadet units[45] and a £4 million allocation to the DoE Scheme (see Chap. 3).

Nonetheless, 'traditional' voluntary youth organisations such as these often found themselves in this period having in effect to compete for still scarce public resources as both central government and some local councils began proactively to encourage and indeed fund two newer 'voluntary' youth initiatives—the NCS and the OnSide Youth Zones.

## THE NATIONAL CITIZENS SERVICE

The NCS, founded in 2011, has to be regarded as to a significant extent a state-provided service given that, as it acknowledged in 2023, it was by then being '… funded by the UK Government … as a core part of the National Youth Guarantee'[46] (see Chaps. 3 and 9).

However, as it has continued to operate as a trust and a (self-described) 'Arms Length Body', it also, somewhat contradictorily, has to be treated as a youth sector voluntary organisation.

With 'underserved groups or those who the existing program did not reach' at its targets,[47] from January 2023, NCS 'redesigned' its previous four-week programme. The choice for young people was extended so that, as well as a residential experience, this now also offered community-based activities and/or online learning. Backed by a £20 million fund, it came, too, with two-year grants for local groups for '… delivering community experiences … (both) open to all and targeted to specific groups'.[48] In its business plan for 2023–24 published the following May,[49] all this was located in what it called the 'significant once-in-a-generation disruptions, caused by the COVID-19 pandemic, Brexit, and … the Russian invasion of Ukraine' and later by the cost-of-living crisis.

In the plan, NCS outlined its overall vision as to 'support (young people) to become world ready and work ready—through growing their

[45] Fiona Simpson, 2021, 'DfE announces £1m boost for school-based cadet units', *CYPN*, 7 April.

[46] NCS Trust, 2023, *Annual Business Plan 2023/24*, DCMS, 24 May, https://www.gov.uk/government/publications/national-citizen-service-trust-annual-business-plan-2023-to-2024.

[47] NCS Trust, 2023, *Annual Business Plan 2023/24*, p. 8.

[48] Joe Lepper, 2023, 'Revamped social action scheme sees NCS aim for greater impact', *CYPN*, 3 January.

[49] NCS Trust, 2023, *Annual Business Plan 2023/24*.

confidence, independence and skills', having '… resilience and wellbeing', 'an impact on the world' and 'respect and tolerance for difference and diversity'. These aspirations were to be achieved by, for example, 'provid(ing) opportunities for volunteering and social action' and 'enabl(ing) social mixing'. Its strategic priorities for the year were listed as to

- *Demonstrate impact and prepare for the future*
- *Provide a new NCS offer for young people*
- *Build external partnerships and positive collaboration*
- *Operate as an inclusive and agile Trust*

In response to the new pressures on young people caused by those wider 'disruptions', the plan also recorded that since its launch in 2021, NCS Connect had 'engaged over 60,000 young people in articles, features and stories about preparing for a post-pandemic world' and that the new two-week format's return to in-person residential experiences had by 2022 'reduced costs whilst improving accessibility'.

By the time NCS published its Annual Report for 2022–23 in December 2023,[50] it was recording the involvement of over 120,000 young people in 'an NCS experience'. On the summer and autumn programmes, they included 21 per cent eligible for free school meals, 9 per cent who had had a Special Educational Needs and Disability (SEND) and Educational, Health and Care (EHC) plan and 33 per cent from Black, Asian and minority ethnic backgrounds. (These figures compared, respectively, with 19 per cent, 2 per cent and 26 per cent of state secondary school pupils overall.) More young people had also connected with NCS's online network, with 101,148 engaged with content on its blog compared with 62,543 in the previous year. Also tracked were the programme's impacts on, for example, participants' employability, their likelihood of 'engaging in volunteering and/or social action' and their more positive feelings about people from different backgrounds.

The report also outlined preparation for a new NCS strategy and offer for 2023–25 involving a 'new delivery model for commissioning experiences through both contracting and grant funding'. This would result in

---

[50] NCS Trust, 2023, *Annual Report 2022–23*, DCMS, 7 December, https://assets.publishing.service.gov.uk/media/6572e6c233b7f20012b720c6/E03008536_National_Citizen_Service_Trust_ARA_22-23_Web_Accessible.pdf.

NCS working with 'over 300 partners to deliver a range of experiences' as well as plans to 'build capabilities and strengthen collaboration with the (wider) youth sector'.

Clearly, these opportunities and the stretching personal and group experiences they could provide were likely to be welcomed and valued by many young people. From an open youth work perspective, however, the Scheme had two significant limitations. One was that its programmes were still open only to 16- and 17-year-olds; the other was that it clearly wasn't designed or resourced to fill the gap left by the loss since 2010 of all those locally based and accessible drop-in leisure facilities which, according to a 2013 NCVYS report were then being used by approximately one million 8–25-year-olds.[51]

## ONSIDE YOUTH ZONES

When businessman Bill Holroyd took over as Chair of the Bolton Lads and Girls Club in 2006, he quickly concluded that this 130-year-old organisation could be a model for a significant new development across the voluntary youth sector.[52] The result was OnSide which, registered as a charity in 2008, had by mid-2023 raised £118 million to set up a 'network' of 18 'Youth Zones' in the UK and another £11 million to support their ongoing programmes. In the process, 1550 new jobs and volunteering opportunities had been created, and 483 workers and volunteers had been trained on OnSide's 'bespoke training programme—the Talent Academy'.[53]

### From 'Vision', 'Standards' and 'Mission' …

Underpinned by 'shared standards' including 'championing' the power of the practice, this growth was driven by a 'vision' of 'empower(ing) young people to lead positive fulfilling lives by providing access to incredible spaces and excellent youth work, delivered by outstanding people, where

[51] National Council for Voluntary Youth Services, *Youth Report 2013*, NCYVS, p. 2.
[52] OnSide, 'About OnSide', https://www.onsideyouthzones.org/about-onside/, accessed December 2022.
[53] OnSide, 2023, *Here for Young People*, https://www.onsideyouthzones.org//content/uploads/2021/09/40132-OnSide-New-About-Us-doc_V39.pdf, p. 7, accessed May 2023.

they are needed the most'.[54] By 'leading and supporting the development and sustainment of high-quality youth work at scale in many towns and cities', it thus sought to enable

> *... thousands of young people ... (to) have a place where they can go, be safe, meet friends, get active, feel at home, be supported when experiencing challenges, learn new skills, enjoy themselves and be inspired.*[55]

### ... To Programmes, Projects—And Users?

Examples of how these aspirations have been and are still being implemented have included promises that, for example, the Bristol Zone will offer more than 20 activities every evening including 'employability training', and that the Crewe Zone will have a wide range of sports and arts facilities including a recording studio and rooftop 'kick pitch'.[56]

More broadly, OnSide has sought to achieve its goals through:

- A 'Stronger Sisters' programme, aimed at 'helping to raise aspirations through sharing experiences and building strong support networks'.[57]
- A 'Culture of Health' project with long-term aims described as 'to embed a culture of health and wellbeing in all Youth Zones, including training staff to better support young people and each other'.[58]
- A 'Get a Job' project to help prepare young people to move into employment, education or training.[59]
- An 'Active Youth' project funded by UK Youth, providing 'sports sessions targeted at inactive young people, with opportunities for Young Leaders to shine'.[60]

[54] OnSide, 2021, *Strategic Plan 2021–2024*, November, p. 3, https://www.onsideyouth-zones.org/news/onside-launches-new-strategic-plan/; OnSide, 2023, *Here for Young People*, p. 3.

[55] OnSide, 2021, *Here for Young People: Annual Review 2020–2021*, p. 28, 16 December 2022, https://www.onsideyouthzones.org//content/uploads/2022/11/OnSide_Annual-review-FINAL.pdf, accessed September 2022.

[56] Emily Harle, 2023, 'Thousands of young people to benefit as youth clubs approved', *CYPN*, 30 June.

[57] See https://www.onsideyouthzones.org/?s=Stronger+sister.

[58] https://www.onsideyouthzones.org/?s=Culture+of+Health.

[59] onsideyouthzones.org/?s=Get+a+Job.

[60] onsideyouthzones.org/?s=Active+Youth.

OnSide has defined its target group as 'local young people ... between eight and 19, or up to 25 with a disability'.[61] By mid-2023, 50,000 had been recorded as having made 650,000 'visits' to the Zones across the country, with, for example, 4000 from south Bristol predicted to sign up for its Zone when it opened in 2025.[62]

Clearly crucial to mounting and delivering, this face-to-face work has been the organisation's commitment to '… strengthen relationships with government and the youth sector'. In 2021, as well as partnering with the Back Youth Alliance and the National Youth Advisory Board,[63] it was working with King's College London's 'Evidence Development and Incubation Team' (EDIT) 'to revise (its) evaluation framework ... and to develop robust outcome measures'.[64] These now include a range of feedback 'stories' from young people and from 'supporters' in partner organisations.[65]

### *Funding*

To '… sustain delivery for the long term', OnSide has drawn on what it has called 'our unique private sector input and a diverse range of funding' which has included the Youth Investment Fund (see Chap. 3), the National Lottery and trusts and foundations.[66] In a period when they have continued to struggle to find resources to reinstate Youth Service facilities lost during austerity, local authorities have nonetheless also made significant financial inputs to OnSide developments. These have, for example, included:

---

[61] OnSide, 'The Way Forward for Youth Provision', https://www.onsideyouthzones.org/content/uploads/2018/09/OnSide-Youth-Zones-The-Way-Forward.pdf, p. 2, accessed May 2023.

[62] OnSide, 2023, *Here for Young People*, p. 7, accessed May 2023; Emily Harle, 2023, 'Thousands of young people to benefit as youth clubs approved', *CYPN*, 30 June.

[63] OnSide, 2021, *Here for Young People: Annual Review 2020–2021*, p. 11.

[64] OnSide, 2021, *Here for Young People: Annual Review 2020–2021*, p. 9.

[65] OnSide, 'Impact Stories', https://www.onsideyouthzones.org/impact/impact-stories/, accessed May 2023.

[66] Neil Puffett, 2019, 'Government announces money for new youth zone' *CYPN*, 16 August; Joe Lepper, 2022, 'Historic warehouses to be turned into youth club following £2.7m grant, *CYPN*, 3 February; OnSide, 2021, *Strategic Plan 2021–2024*, p. 3; OnSide, 2021, *Here for Young People: Annual Review 2020–2021*, p. 31; Emily Harle, 2023, 'Thousands of young people to benefit as youth clubs approved', *CYPN*, 30 June.

- £4.1 million by Basildon Council and £4.5 million by Barnsley Council towards Youth Zone construction costs in their areas.[67]
- £4.2 million by Bristol Council towards construction costs and a pledge of £400,000 a year for annual running costs.[68]
- £300,000 from Croydon Council for running costs for the three years to 2021.[69]
- Cheshire East and local town council contributions towards the construction and running costs of a Youth Zone in Crewe.[70]

### Some Questions

Clearly for many young people, having access to such high-quality arts, sports, IT and other facilities has opened up new much-needed developmental opportunities, especially in areas—urban as well as rural—where these are scarce or non-existent. Nonetheless, from an open youth work perspective, there are questions here, too, which merit some further exploration.

One is: for how many of the thousands—*thousands*—of the young people coming through the Youth Zones' doors is the OnSide promise of providing 'dedicated youth worker support' being achieved? That is, how far, for how many of those users, is the worker-young person relationship developed and shaped by the 'on-the-wing', young people-led, process-driven features which define open youth work practice? (see Preface). Though on this OnSide has offered two indirect responses, these provide only limited evidence: that, for example, the Zones 'aren't youth centres as you may know them'[71] and that in 2021–22, 23 of its workers gained the Level 3 Youth Work Diploma.[72]

---

[67] Fiona Simpson, 2020,'Essex first OnSide youth zone given green light,' *CYPN*, 26 November; Fiona Simpson, 2021, 'Barnsley gives go-ahead to Yorkshire's first youth zone' *CYPN*, 18 August.

[68] Fiona Simpson, 2021, ' Green light for South West's first Youth Zone', *CYPN* 22 September.

[69] Fiona Simpson, 2021, 'Legacy Youth Zone launches major fundraising drive', *CYPN*, 25 November.

[70] Emily Harle, 2023, 'Thousands of young people to benefit as youth clubs approved', *CYPN*, 30 June.

[71] OnSide, 2023, *Here for Young People*, p. 4, accessed May 2023.

[72] OnSide, 2021, *Here for Young People: Annual Review 2020–2021*, p. 21. See also Gaby Hinsliff, 2024, 'Not Going Out', *Guardian Saturday*, 10 Feb. 24.

Related questions emerge, too, when the OnSide approach is considered in relation to the academics' proposals in the 2021 DCMS *Youth Review* for 'small-scale, flexible and locally determined' facilities such as 'pop-up or modular builds' (see Chap. 9). Suggesting very different forms of both capital expenditure and face-to-face practice from the OnSide model, these seem to point more, for example, to a youth café in a renovated local shop staffed by youth workers or to detached youth work sessions focused around a youth shelter in a local park.

For young people who might still be testing out whether they want to become involved in an open youth work setting, these kinds of spaces could be particularly attractive and accessible. However, a similar question to that raised at the end of Chap. 5 also seems relevant here: How impressed by 'small-scale' proposals of this kind would local councillors and their officers be if, via a sophisticated PR presentation, substantial additional funding was on offer for setting up a 'high quality' 'state-of-the-art' Youth Zone in their town centre?

# CHAPTER 7

# The Role of the National Youth Agency

**Abstract** The NYA sought to implement its self-defined role as 'the lead expert and national body for youth work' in this period by setting out a Strategic Plan, a 'ten-year vision' and a Roadmap to a National Youth Strategy—initiatives which illustrated how 'youth work' was able to address both young people's personal needs and their wider societal challenges. In addition to its key role in developing and approving training routes into youth work (considered in detail in Chap. 8), other NYA proposals and interventions focused on safeguarding in youth work, the commissioning of youth work provision, developing a national youth work curriculum, clarifying local authorities' statutory guidance and on the sector's financial pressures. The Agency also carried out youth sector censuses and responded to the impacts on young people of the pandemic, the cost-of-living crisis and county lines exploitation.

**Keywords** Safeguarding • Commissioning • Youth work curriculum • Statutory guidance • Financial pressures • Youth sector censuses • National Youth Strategy

## Youth Work's 'Lead Expert and National Body'

In an interview in 2017 shortly after his appointment as 'managing director' (now Chief Executive),[1] Leigh Middleton set out his top three priorities for the NYA as follows:

- Developing '… further commercial work' by extending to 'four or five more … programmes' NYA's corporate sponsorship relationship with the telecommunications company O2.
- The 'professional development of the sector'—considered in detail in Chap. 8.
- 'Policy development work'.

A leaflet published in 2019 or 2020[2] expanded on the last priority to cover 'Strategic service review and development', 'Workforce development …', 'Influencing practice through policy and research', 'Programme design and management', 'Quality frameworks and consultation' and 'Research and evaluation'.

Describing the Agency as 'agile, creative and driven', the leaflet committed it to '… looking to all corners of the funding world to secure support not only for NYA activity but … for partner organisations'. It also defined its wider organisational role as '… (the) lead expert and national body for youth work in England'—later explained more formally as the 'Professional Statutory and Regulatory Body for youth work in England'.[3]

## Implementing the 'Lead Role'

### An NYA Strategic Plan

In March 2020, the NYA set out its Strategic Plan, to run to 2025.[4] Starting with a brief reminder of its 50+ year history, this referenced both

---

[1] Neil Puffett, 2017, 'Steering youth work's future: Leigh Middleton, Managing Director, National Youth Agency', *CYPN*, 26 September.

[2] NYA, undated, 'Youth Work: Transforming the lives of young people'.

[3] See, for example, https://www.nya.org.uk/about-us/#:~:text=NYA%20is%20the%20national%20body,for%20youth%20work%20in%20England.

[4] NYA, 2020, 'Our Strategic Plan 2020 to 2025', https://s3.eu-west-1.amazonaws.com/assets.nya2.joltrouter.net/wp-content/uploads/20210517090231/1026-NYA-Strategy-2020_25-P7.pdf, accessed 8 February 2024.

its government funding and 'other diverse funding to deliver programmes which support our wider charitable mission ...' Three forms of 'essential guidance, resources and support' already being provided or planned were listed:

- 'Dedicated Covid-19 guidance ... during 2020'.
- A 'National Youth Work Curriculum' (examined below).
- A 'Research Hub (which) has published valuable reports to inform the sector's operational and strategic development, including advocacy and influence with government and commissioners'.

After diagrammatically setting out its 'strategic goals', the plan outlined its intended 'Impact', a three-stepped 'Theory of Change' and its intended outcomes, with the latter explained as 'those set on the Centre for Youth Impact's Outcome Framework'. Under the general headings of 'Stakeholders', 'Competences' and 'People' and 'Resources', its remaining 25 pages outlined 20 'Objectives' which included 'creat(ing) Impactful Youth Work Opportunities for Young People'; being 'innovative and efficient with robust governance' and 'increas(ing) diversity and perspectives of the youth sector'.

### A Ten-Year Vision for Youth Work

In the spring of 2021, the NYA published the final version of a ten-year vision for youth work.[5] At its heart were the goals of 'all young people having access to quality youth work and youth services', of youth work being 'recognised as a distinct form of education' and of the 'mobilisation and the professional development of youth work'. Seen as essential for realising these were

- *A clear, statutory basis ... to ensure a base-level of open-access youth services.*
- *'... a target within in each secondary school catchment area of two full-time equivalent professional, JNC (Joint Negotiating Committee)*

---

[5] NYA, 2021, 'Ten Year Vision for Youth Work 2020–2030', Spring, https://www.nya.org.uk/resource/10-year-vision-for-youth-work/; Derren Hayes, 2020, 'NYA Guidance offers blueprint to revitalise youth work services', *CYPN*, 27 October.

*qualified youth workers and a team of at least four youth support workers alongside trained volunteers.*

- *... additional provision of detached and outreach youth work, digitalised youth work and transport where needed to access opportunities.*
- *... young people ... (to be) involved to co-design and develop services in their locality.*
- *A realignment of £1.2bn annual funding (adjusted for inflation) from government ring-fenced for open-access youth services ...*
- *... a major capital building programme ...'*

For implementation at the organisational level, the paper suggested there would need to be

- *... a diverse range of providers as a flourishing eco-system of community-based youth work.*
- *Local youth partnerships to bring together the public, private, voluntary and community sector to make the most effective use of all available funding and assets.*
- *Increased levels of democratic engagement and young people actively involved in community leadership roles and decision-making across services and organisations.*
- *Digital literacy and an end to digital poverty.*

For the on-the-ground practice to be able to deliver the vision it also proposed

- *... the recruitment and training of 10,000 qualified youth workers;*
- *... a bursary programme for entry-level training for 20,000 youth support workers;*
- *... increased volunteering;*
- *A Youth Covenant for ... shared outcomes across funders, commissioners and services.*

## A Roadmap to a National Youth Strategy

In October 2023, supported by 'twenty leading youth sector organisations', the NYA published a 'Roadmap to a National Youth Strategy[6] developed, it said, by the National Youth Sector Advisory Board (NYSAB).[7] This it described as 'a forum for policy and practice for the youth sector' whose aims included 'to engage government and policymakers and to inform the professional, statutory and regulatory role of the National Youth Agency as the national standards body for youth work in England'. Working through what it called 'the extended networks of (NYA) members, consultation, and wider sector engagement', the Board's task was defined as '… to gather and present collective insights and strategic direction for the sector as a whole, across statutory and voluntary youth services, and related professions'.[8]

A key aim of the Roadmap was to 'rebuild the youth sector' so that

> … all young people can access quality youth work to promote their mental health and wellbeing, develop their life skills, help them have a voice on decisions that affect them and realise their full potential.

To achieve this, the Roadmap recommended that the national government

> … bring about a step-change in the way that youth work is recognised and … get youth work better integrated into local strategies and multi-agency pathways to support young people.

Also recommended was that the government

---

[6] NYA, 2023, 'Leading youth sector organisations call for a Roadmap to a National Youth Strategy', 2 October; https://www.nya.org.uk/leading-youth-sector-organisations-call-for-roadmap-to-a-national-youth-strategy/#:~:text=The%20Roadmap%2C%20which%20has%20been,that%20affect%20them%20and%20realise; NYA, 2023, 'Roadmap to a National Youth Strategy', October, https://www.s3.eu-west-1.amazonaws.com/assets.nya2.joltrouter.net/wp-content/uploads/2023/11/01165048/Roadmap-to-national-youth-strategy-DIGITAL.pdf.

[7] NYA, 'National Youth Sector Advisory Board (NYSAB)', https://www.nya.org.uk/nysab/, accessed 8 February 2024.

[8] NYA, 2023, 'Leading youth sector organisations call for a Roadmap to a National Youth Strategy', 2 October.

- Guarantee long-term funding and other resourcing so that local authorities could fulfil their (now strengthened) statutory duty to provide the youth work facilities;
- Upskill the existing workforce, particularly by providing more training for volunteers;
- Attract more new entrants to the youth sector.

## PROGRAMMES AND PROJECTS

To implement its vision, Strategy and the Roadmap, the NYA took a range of sometimes ambitious policy- and practice-focused initiatives. With the training and qualifications routes which are examined in detail in Chap. 8 as a particularly high priority, these not only prompted and scrutinised new developments within youth work itself. They also extended into the broader fields of 'youth services' and youth policy by carrying out reviews, surveys and research and by proposing how youth work could help address the problems then facing young people.[9]

Recognition of this wider role came in October 2020 when one of its projects—Routes to Success—was awarded £300,000 by the National Lottery Community Fund.[10] Over the following six months, the money was to be used in two ways. One was to support the delivery of activities through the Covid crisis by providing youth workers with relevant training, practice development skills and open-access podcasts; the other was to help sector organisations manage risk during lockdowns by offering 'development tools' and 'bespoke support'. These inputs were underpinned by an NYA guidance paper, updated for use in England from April 2022, on 'managing youth sector activities and spaces during Covid-19'.[11]

As well as news and information on relevant youth work and youth services developments, the NYA website offered links to a range of other resources.[12] Under the heading 'Transforming the lives of young people through the power of youth work', these included

[9] See, for example, NYA, 2023, *Better Together: Youth work in schools – Complementing formal education to change young people's lives*, June, https://www.nya.org.uk/youth-work-with-schools/; Emily Harle, 2023, 'Youth work in schools key to improving attendance rates, NYA inquiry finds', *CYPN*, 21 June.

[10] NYA, 2020, 'NYA awarded National Lottery Funding for Covid-19 Project', 7 October, https://www.nya.org.uk/nlf-funded/.

[11] See https://www.nya.org.uk/guidance/ accessed 18 January 2023.

[12] See https://www.nya.org.uk/.

- An 'NYA Academy' whose aim was 'to enhance the skills of Youth Work practitioners through our dedicated online learning platform'.[13]
- An NYA Quality Mark intended to encourage organisations to 'reflect on and review the services they offered young people and so provide youth work to the best possible standard'.[14] The first award announced in March 2023 was to the Creative Youth Network based in the South West—judged as 'outstanding' for

*... its progressive approach to widening participation of young people across the organisation as well as its proven track record in co-designing programmes that recognise—and act upon—the needs and interests of the region's many diverse communities.*[15]

- Amplifi—'an online personal development platform designed for young people, by young people'.[16]
- Hear by Right—'an organisational development tool ... supporting organisations to plan, develop and evaluate their participation practices and provision, keeping young people at the heart of decision making whilst increasing their voice, influence and place within society'.[17]
- An annual 'Youth Work Week' which in November 2023, entitled 'Youth work in every place and space', included six young people's 'case studies'.[18]
- Other online and in-person events including 'Youth work tea breaks'; NYA supper clubs'; Regional Roadshows; Youth Work Connect sessions, one of which in early 2024 focused on misogyny[19] and sessions on 'Connecting Youth Services to their Local McDonalds'.
- A link to its 'NatWest Thrive with a Marcus Rashford' programme which had been 'developed by specialist youth workers at the National Youth Agency working closely with young people'. This

[13] Available at https://www.nya.org.uk/skills/academy/.

[14] Available at https://www.nya.org.uk/quality/quality-mark/.

[15] Joe Lepper, 2023, 'Support charity first to receive prestigious youth services award' *CYPN*, 22 March.

[16] Accessed 8 February 2024 via https://www.nya.org.uk/nya-launch-new-digital-hub-to-help-young-people-power-forwards-to-a-bright-future-in-learning-and-work/.

[17] Available at https://www.nya.org.uk/resource/hear-by-right/.

[18] NYA, 2023, 'Youth Work Week 2023', https://www.nya.org.uk/skills/yww/#:~:text=Join%20us%20from%20Monday%206,for%20Youth%20Work%20Week%202023.

[19] NYA email, 6 February 2024.

was described as for 'young people between the ages of 8 and 24 years to develop their self-belief, identify their passions and build up the skills they need to become who they want to be'. More specific programme focuses were on 'young people learning life skills, developing a positive money mindset and how to set goals and identify the steps to achieving them'.[20] A digital version of the programme was launched in September 2023 comprising six downloadable modules 'offering FREE ready-to-use youth work sessions to help enhance your youth work offer this autumn'.[21]

Supporting these efforts, too, was a regular release of papers with focuses falling under three broad headings: clarifying and developing NYA's own role and intended impact; monitoring and further developing youth work practice; and key issues and concerns affecting young people.

## Monitoring and Developing Youth Work Practice

### Safeguarding and Risk Management

In April 2021, in part prompted by pandemic pressures and following discussions with the National Society for the Prevention of Cruelty to Children (NSPCC) and the Youth Safeguarding Forum, the NYA launched a 'safeguarding and risk management hub'.[22] Responding to evidence that only three per cent of the 1000 safeguarding courses it had reviewed were relevant to youth workers, this promised training materials specifically designed for both paid workers and volunteers. It also offered resources to help them protect the young people they were working with focus, for example, on developing safe policies and procedures, whistleblowing, supervision and management. Four 'accredited training opportunities' on offer in January and February 2024 were to address similar safeguarding and risk management issues.

---

[20] Available at https://www.nya.org.uk/natwest-thrive-with-marcus-rashford/, accessed 9 February 2024.

[21] NYA email, 2023, 'NatWest Thrive Online: New Free Digital Resource', 26 September; available at https://www.nya.org.uk/natwest-thrive-online/.

[22] NYA, 2021, 'Safeguarding and Risk Management Hub', https://www.nya.org.uk/skills/safeguarding-and-risk-management-hub/, accessed 3 January 2023 and 9 February 2024; Joe Lepper, 2021, 'NYA launches free safeguarding resources for youth workers', *CYPN*, 29 April.

## Commissioning Procedures

The NYA explained that the *Guide to Commissioning Outcomes for Young People*,[23] published in 2019, was needed because, as by then local authorities were co-ordinators rather than direct providers of local youth work facilities (see Chap. 4), they needed to have effective commissioning procedures. It located this need more specifically in two high priority 'current concerns': 'knife crime, poor mental health and the exploitation of young people by adults', and '... the continued contraction of local authority youth services'. Both these developments, it concluded, had left 'the relevance of youth work ... not clear enough'.

In seeking clarification of the role of youth work, it drew on the definition adopted by the APPG report on youth affairs, jointly signed off by the Committee Chair and Leigh Middleton and published by the NYA in April 2019.[24] This explained the practice as

> ... *provid(ing) non-formal education that focuses on the personal and social development of participants. Uniquely it does this through engagement with young people's culture and their community ... Many young people engage in youth work because it feels different from school and is therefore capable of reaching individuals and communities who may otherwise not engage.*

In addressing 'a number of contemporary commissioning challenges faced by local authorities ... where youth work could deliver the intended outcomes', the NYA paper started from three questions: What is youth work? How does it work? And what are its benefits? It sought particularly to 'demonstrate how to involve young people in the commissioning process from end to end'—including by charities and what it called 'social businesses'. Albeit implicitly, section headings such as 'How to engage the youth market', 'Outcome-based contracting and Social Impact Bonds' and 'An outcomes framework for young people' also reflected the continuing influence here, too, of some neo-liberal ways of framing the issues to be addressed.

[23] NYA, 2019, 'A guide to commissioning outcomes for young people', https://static.nya.org.uk/static/12e22e24ea219ecfc09405f1d2f814cc/NYA-Commissioning-report-FINAL-lowres.pdf.

[24] APPG, 2019, *Youth Work Inquiry: Final Report,* NYA, April, p. 10, https://s3.eu-west-1.amazonaws.com/assets.nya2.joltrouter.net/wp-content/uploads/20210417221107/APPG-Youth-Work-Inquiry-Final-Report-April-2019-ONLINE.pdf.

## *A National Youth Work Curriculum?*

During this period, one especially significant intervention by the NYA into youth work thinking and practice was its publication in September 2020 of a 'National Curriculum for Youth Work'.[25] Its purpose was explained as

> ... *to enable a greater understanding of youth work practice, provide an educational framework and act as a reference tool to be used by decision-makers, policy-makers, commissioners, youth workers and young people.*

In effect distancing itself from the broadened conception of 'youth work' adopted in other of its and Middleton's statements (see Chap. 5), a key proposition on which the proposed curriculum rested was that

> ... *youth work ... differs from other services in that it is voluntary for young people to engage ..., and the process starts from where the young people are at, their interests, goals and experiences, focussing on personal and social development through a strength-based (asset) approach.*

Capturing a phrase used in the Open Letter which launched the In Defence of Youth Work campaign in 2009,[26] key elements of the NYA's 30-page 'Curriculum' document focused on the 'cornerstones of youth work'—defined here as education, empowerment, equality and participation. Also considered in the paper were

- Youth work's values and principles, the youth work process and the relationship of this to 'praxis'. Illustrated by examples of 'projects and activities', these were linked to ten 'youth work themes' such as 'Identity and belonging', 'Health and wellbeing', 'Economic and financial wellbeing' and 'The environment and sustainable development'.
- 'Related professions' whose work 'youth work complements and can support'—identified as teaching, social care, health and youth justice.

[25] NYA, 2020, 'National Youth Work Curriculum', Version 1, September, https://s3.eu-west-1.amazonaws.com/assets.nya2.joltrouter.net/wp-content/uploads/20210414232918/5.3.1-0923-NYA-Youth-Work-Curriculum-DIGITAL1.pdf, accessed 9 February 2024.
[26] IDYW, 2009, 'The Open Letter', https://indefenceofyouthwork.com/the-in-defence-of-youth-work-letter-2/.

- Documents which 'underpinned, informed and supported' a rights-based approach to youth work and provided 'quality standards' for the practice.

The appearance of the proposed curriculum attracted some critical attention—most explicitly in an article by Jon Ord in the October 2020 issue of *Youth and Policy*.[27] Ord's starting proposition was that 'the question for youth work is not whether it has a curriculum but what kind of curriculum it has', including whether, with pre-determined outcomes, it is being imposed from above. Though questioning NYA's failure to consult before publishing its paper, Ord nonetheless affirmed that, rather than being 'product-based' like previous top-down government versions, its proposals were 'process-led': that is, they assumed '... content negotiated with young people and ... outcomes emerg(ing) out of a dynamic unfolding of practice ...'.

Ord did, however, point to one key missing feature in NYA's articulation of this process: 'explicit references to its non-linear nature ...' This, he argued, was '... grounded in (youth work's) dynamic and changeable environment and explains the complex relationship between the interventions by youth workers and the resulting outcomes'.

### Statutory Guidance for Local Authorities

A month after publishing its curriculum document, the NYA released a first version of a paper focused on clarifying and making more effective English local authorities' statutory duties to provide open youth work facilities.[28] It was framed overall by the evidence that, as a result of councils' austerity cuts to young people's services, 'the standard (youth work) model has been replaced by a patchwork of different approaches with, for example, some councils providing just targeted provision while others contract out delivery to not-for-profit mutuals'.

In his Foreword to the first paper, Leigh Middleton posed four questions for clarifying the steps a local authority could take to fulfil what he

---

[27] Jon Ord, 2020, 'The National Youth Work Curriculum: A process-based curriculum?', *Youth and Policy*, 5 October, https://www.youthandpolicy.org/articles/the-national-youth-work-curriculum/.

[28] Derren Hayes, 2020, 'NYA Guidance offers blueprint to revitalise youth work services', *CYPN*, 27 October; Fiona Simpson, 2020, 'NYA publishes new youth work guidance for local authorities', *CYPN*, 30 October.

was now calling 'its statutory duty to improve young people's well-being ...':

- *What is expected of local authorities?*
- *What should the local offer (of activities and facilities) look like?*
- *What needs to be done?*
- *Why youth work?*

Advocating an 'access for all' approach to an expanded age group of 8–24-year-olds, the NYA paper then summarised seven ways in which local authorities could—should—carry out their duties. These, for example, included

- *... secur(ing) sufficient youth services in their area;*
- *Universal, open access youth services (which) ensure a base-level of quality provision for all young people;*
- *... an annual plan to ensure open access and accountability ...;*
- *... the active involvement of young people in decision-making.*

For ensuring the necessary access for '"qualifying young persons" in its area', it particularly highlighted a local authority's requirement to provide

(a) *Sufficient educational leisure-time activities which are for the improvement of their well-being, and sufficient facilities for such activities and*
(b) *Sufficient recreational leisure-time activities which are for the improvement of their well-being, and sufficient facilities for such activities.*

The paper later again explained this more specifically by restating its proposal that, in each secondary school catchment area, services locate at least two full-time equivalent JNC-qualified 'professional' youth workers, at least four youth support workers and trained volunteers.

Councils were also offered advice on how to negotiate the guidance's references to 'reasonable and practical implementation'—a clause which during the austerity decade was used by many councils to justify major cuts to their youth services (see Chaps. 3 and 9). Though the NYA paper at no point advocated that the clause be removed or even significantly amended, it did stress that 'there should only be exceptional circumstances where it is not practicable for local authorities to secure services due to insufficient "capabilities and other priorities"'. It recommended, too, that 'Government be prepared to intervene where services are not functioning at a sufficient level by providing the resources for ensuring that a provision is sustainable'. In its final main section, the paper also set out eight 'guiding principles' focused, for example, on the need for planning with other agencies, for services to be 'easily available via universal, open-access settings' and for 'active involvement from young people in the co-production of services'.

A later version of the paper[29] had an added section focused specifically on 'The Impact of COVID-19'. This noted how the pandemic had 'exacerbated the challenges faced by young people' and that 'the loss or reduction of youth services in local authority areas across the country ... has been identified as a factor in young people's declining wellbeing'. A priority for all local authorities was therefore seen as '... to strengthen and maintain youth services' with 'robust data support(ing) a public health approach ...'

In response to the guidance to local authorities finally released by the DCMS in September 2023 (see Chap. 9),[30] the NYA published a 58-page 'Toolkit' intended 'to support council officials, elected members, funders and partners'.[31] This provided what it called 'the core of a suite of documents and resources available from the NYA' which 'set out the standards, frameworks, factors and steps local authorities should consider when developing their local youth offer'. It particularly encouraged local authorities to evaluate how their current youth work offer met nine 'essentials' seen as integral to enabling them to secure a local youth offer in compliance with their statutory duty.

---

[29] NYA, 2020, 'Guidance for Local Authorities on Providing Youth Services, p4, October, https://nya.org.uk/new-national-guidance-for-local-authorities-on-providing-youth-services/

[30] GOV.UK, 2023, 'Statutory guidance for local authorities on services to improve young people's well being', https://www.gov.uk/government/publications/statutory-guidance-for-local-authorities-youth-provision/statutory-guidance-for-local-authorities-on-services-to-improve-young-peoples-well-being, 23 September.

[31] NYA, undated, *How to fulfil Your Statutory Duties under Section 507B of the Education Act,* https://s3.eu-west-1.amazonaws.com/assets.nya2.joltrouter.net/wp-content/uploads/2023/09/29102527/NYA_How-to-fulfil-your-Statutory-Duty-A-toolkit-for-local-authorities-1.pdf.

## *Youth Charities Running on Empty; Youth Services Under Threat*

Two NYA papers published nearly a year apart brought together the evidence then emerging of the financial pressures youth work organisations were facing as a result of the Covid pandemic. The first, 'Running on Empty'[32] released in November 2020, warned that, with 'central government … sat on a £500 million new Youth Investment Fund' (see Chap. 3) and funding for the NCS ring-fenced to 2022–23, 'loss of funding and job cuts will see the closure of youth services through the winter …'.

Specific examples of these pressures included

- '1 in 4 youth charities will not be able to meet their running costs, in the run up to Christmas'.
- '1in 2 will not be able to meet operational costs within 12 months'.
- '7 in 10 have lost staff capacity; with 1 in 10 set to make staff redundant this year'.

It also cautioned that 'without staff support and resources, the volunteer base will fall away' and assumed 'a further round of cuts … from local authority youth services'.

The second report,[33] released in September 2021 in collaboration with the YMCA, was tellingly entitled 'Time's Running Out'. Further highlighting the threats to youth work providers, it, for example, revealed that 23 per cent of the organisations surveyed were reporting fewer than six months of reserves and that a further third (35 per cent) were expecting to be able to operate normally for only between six months and a year. Pointing also to findings that 'for every £16 cut from all local services by local authorities, £1 has fallen on youth provision', the report described what was happening as 'a postcode lottery of service for young people'. This was illustrated by a cut in total youth service spending in deprived areas of around £90 per head compared with just around £50 in the most affluent areas. Added to this by then was a 'shortfall of at least 40,000 adult volunteers'—all at a time when 'the number of vulnerable young

---

[32] NYA, 2020, 'Youth charities are "running on empty"', November, https://www.nya.org.uk/resource/youth-charities-are-running-on-empty/.

[33] NYA/YMCA, 2021, 'Time's Running Out: Youth services under threat and lost opportunities for young people', NYA September, https://www.nya.org.uk/youth-services-are-in-crisis-failure-to-act-now-will-see-lost-opportunities-for-young-people/.

people (aged 8–19 year olds) in England rose from an estimated 1 million up to 3 million'.

In response, the report recommended a range of measures including 'strengthening statutory guidance for local authorities'; the immediate release of the promised money from the Youth Investment Fund; and 'long term investment from the government's (planned) spending review and grants settlements' in order particularly to recruit and train more youth workers. The latter proposal did eventually get some government recognition through the funding it provided for youth work training bursaries[34] (see Chap. 8).

### 'Overlooked' Rural Areas

Another of the NYA papers published at this time—'Overlooked: Young People and Rural Services'[35]—compared youth work provision in rural and urban areas. Its key overall conclusion was that

> … for many young people, living in a rural community means lack of facilities, such as clubs … This isolation is exacerbated by a lack of transport options and hidden, rural poverty.

NYA's response here was to recommend '… a rural action plan for youth services, designed with young people'. This, it said, should include

- … a comprehensive map of youth services and out of school activities in rural areas;
- Youth services … planned and delivered through local youth partnerships;
- More community transport options;
- Access to free data … (to) bridge the digital divide.

---

[34] Fiona Simpson, 2022, 'NYA launches new round of training bursaries', *CYPN*, 9 March; Emily Harle, 2023, 'NYA launches hundreds of free youth work training places' *CYPN*, 8 February; NYA, undated, 'Funding for youth work training bursaries in 2024', https://www.nya.org.uk/youth-work-bursaries-2024/#:~:text=Up%20to%20five%20hundred%20bursaries,NYA)%20and%20its%20regional%20partners.

[35] NYA, 2021, 'Overlooked: Young people and rural services', August, https://www.nya.org.uk/resource/overlooked-young-people-and-rural-services/.

To help 'unlock and release funding', it also again proposed 'strengthen(ing) statutory guidance for local authorities and funding to secure a baseline for youth provision including detached and mobile youth work ...'

### A National Youth Sector Census

The NYA built up its evidence base for its proposals by carrying out its own 'National Youth Sector Census' in 2021 and again in 2022. Leigh Middleton explained the aim of the first Census as to 'provide essential information to plan, invest and support the youth sector'.[36] Expanding on this in his Foreword to the second report, he described the Census as

> ... an initial two-year programme of research and data analysis, on priority areas for young people and youth work in England ... (S)uch provision is defined as out of school activities that purposefully develop personal and social skills ... where their attendance is voluntary.[37]

He also noted that, though 'the needs and expectations of young people are similar across the country ... what remains perhaps the biggest challenge is equitable access to youth work'.

Findings from the first Census evidencing this challenge included that

- '... (there was) twice as much provision in the most affluent areas as opposed to the most deprived', with '... twice as many buildings purpose-built for, or dedicated towards, young people in affluent areas';
- '... the units of national uniformed organisations, especially those affiliated to Scouts and Girlguiding, ... made up 90% of all (the identified) provision';

---

[36] NYA, 2021, 'Initial Summary of Findings from the National Youth Sector Census', 1 November; NYA, 2022, https://www.nya.org.uk/national-youth-sector-census-first-report/, NYA, 2022, 'Delivering youth work in England: National Youth Sector Census, Second Report', October, https://www.nya.org.uk/wp-content/uploads/Census-second-report-oct22.pdf; Leigh Middleton, 2021, 'The National Youth Sector Census and why it is vital to participate', *CYPN*, 20 April.

[37] NYA, 2022, 'Delivering youth work in England: National Youth Sector Census, Second Report', October, https://www.nya.org.uk/wp-content/uploads/Census-second-report-oct22.pdf.

- 'VCS (voluntary and community sector) organisations which are not affiliated to national or uniformed organisations are, conversely, more concentrated in the most deprived postcodes';
- VCS organisations 'are disproportionately providing (and being commissioned by local authorities to provide) universal services, while local authority provision is more focussed on targeted delivery';
- '15% of upper-tier and unitary local authorities ... (said) that they offered no direct delivery ...'.

The second report then focused on the Census's evidence on a number of specific issues including, for example, 'Targeted funding', 'Commissioning and structure', 'Enablers ... and Inhibitors of good practice' and 'Differences by type of area'.

## MONITORING THE CONDITION OF 'YOUTH'—IN THE TIME OF COVID

### *'Vulnerable' Young People*

Another recurring NYA focus in this period was on the pressures facing young people in their daily lives (see Chap. 2). Very early in the pandemic—in April 2020—it, for example, published *Out of Sight*,[38] a paper endorsed by the Children's Commissioner for England on 'vulnerable' young people. Drawing on statistical and other evidence from a wide range of sources, this focused on three groups of 8–19-year-olds seen as particularly in need of safeguarding and support:

- Those whose 'known' vulnerabilities were being amplified by COVID-19 and who met 'the statutory threshold'—such as being known to social services.
- Those—for example, NEET young people and those excluded from school—who were also 'at risk' of vulnerabilities exacerbated by COVID-19 and the resultant (first) lockdown but who didn't meet the statutory threshold.
- Those with 'emerging' vulnerabilities caused or triggered by COVID-19.

[38] *'NYA, 2020, Out of Sight: Vulnerable Young People: COVID-19 Response,* April, https://www.nya.org.uk/resource/out-of-sight-vulnerable-young-people-covid-19-response/.

The report also highlighted the young people—many 'lacking a "safe" space'—for whom there would be other 'urgent' concerns once the lockdown ended. These included the approximately 700,000 already 'missing from education'; the million at risk of domestic abuse; the approximately 1 million with little or no digital access at home; and the nearly half a million who were homeless or living in a 'precarious' housing situation.

These findings were brought together in two tables. One estimated the number of young people facing 12 of the main 'vulnerabilities', and the other pointed to the need for a 'youth work practice response' to these and other conditions. The paper also highlighted that this was the generation who—financially, with reduced employment opportunities and with a consequential increase in mental health problems—would experience Covid's longer-term costs most directly.

The paper explained its recommended youth work response as

> ... *a vital life-line to vulnerable young people, joining in activities without stigma but able to access support, talk to a trusted adult or disclose a problem for help.*

Within this, detached and outreach youth work attracted specific recognition—identified as able 'to engage young people in the community'. So, too, did the 'many youth clubs and services ... rapidly adapting their work to go digital, with activities, groups and support moving online'. Employers and local authorities were thus urged to provide the tools which (subject to risk assessments) would help youth workers adopt these approaches, including offering training for meeting pandemic-induced vulnerabilities such as trauma and bereavement.

The paper also offered two significant warnings into the longer term. One was that 'nationally one in five youth clubs will not re-open, more in some regions'; the other (even more relevant by early 2024—see Epilogue), of 'a threat hanging over non-statutory youth services should austerity measures return post-pandemic'. Coming out of its evidence and analysis, therefore, were the proposals, implemented in January 2021,[39] that youth work be recognised as an 'essential service' and youth workers classified as 'key workers'.

---

[39] See https://www.nya.org.uk/youth-workers-recognised-as-key-workers/.

## *Young People's Health and Wellbeing*

Explicitly presented as 'build(ing) on the insights from the "Out of Sight?" research report', 'Inside Out' published in August 2020[40] was produced jointly by the NYA and Brook, an organisation offering young people clinical sexual health, education and wellbeing services, training and support.[41] Its focus was specifically on the pandemic's effects on young people's physical and emotional health and, with youth workers here too recognised as 'critical workers', on the need for dedicated youth work responses. Arguing for collaborative approaches, the paper included Forewords by the then Children's Commissioner for England and the 'Head of Impact' at Football Beyond Borders. It also acknowledged 'the work and detailed analysis' and 'the insights' of a range of other youth and mental health organisations.

The paper's starting point was again the 'disproportionate impact' of the pandemic on young people—particularly on their health and wellbeing—and how it had 'compounded inequalities that already existed … hit(ting) vulnerable and marginalised groups the hardest'. It quoted evidence that though 'young people's experiences through COVID-19 show remarkable resilience …', a range of concerns had emerged. In the context of 'over one million young people hav(ing) been lost to youth services', these included that

- '… a quarter of the young people surveyed admitted to breaking lockdown to see friends'.
- With 'more young people … feeling more alone and isolated', '… those with higher levels of depression were more likely to break the rules'.
- '… young people and families are not accessing medical advice'—evidenced by 'a reported drop in A&E attendances'.
- Concerns were emerging about 'poor diet and low levels of physical activity'.
- The kinds of 'early unemployment' that young people were already experiencing 'leads to long term poor health outcomes and the relationship with educational levels …'

---

[40] NYA/Brook, 2020, 'Inside Out: Young people's health and wellbeing – A response to Covid-19', NYA, August, https://www.nya.org.uk/inside-out-nya-brook/.

[41] Accessed at https://www.brook.org.uk/, 15 January 2023.

Though, it was acknowledged, 'there is no "quick fix"' to these problems, key requirements were seen as 'the support of skilled and qualified youth workers and an age appropriate response from health professional trained to support adolescents'. Anticipating 'a possible second wave of COVID-19 or local lockdowns', it also (presciently) identified 'an urgent need for local agencies … to focus resources on teenagers at risk of becoming invisible to health and support services'. This needed to include 'significant investment to recruit, train, upskill and support youth workers and health specialists …'

## Young People's Employment—Now and in the Future

Advocating for these kinds of youth work developments was also at the heart of the *Outside Looking In* paper published by NYA in March 2021 in collaboration with Youth Employment UK.[42] Focusing on the impacts of Covid and, by then too, of the wider global deterioration in the young's employment opportunities and prospects, this was again underpinned by a range of research evidence. This included that

- 'Nearly 800,000 vulnerable 16–24 year olds … not in full-time education or employment face significant barriers in work now and when the extended furlough scheme ends in 2021'.
- 'Some 60% of those who had become unemployed through the pandemic are between the ages of 18 and 24 … with one in ten 16 to 24 year olds not having had a paid job outside casual or summer work'.
- 'More than half of under-25s and of over-65s have been either placed on furlough or lost their jobs compared with one-third of other ages'.
- '… the youngest and oldest workers are overrepresented in jobs under the greatest threat …'
- 'Young people … are low on confidence, not knowing what jobs are available and not seen to have the right skills'.

---

[42] Youth Employment UK/NYA, 2021, 'Outside, Looking In: Young people's employment and the future economy – A youth work response', March, https://static.nya.org.uk/static/51ae026dd2e3835a2a9bc310dd9803c1/1013-NYA-employment-report-Digital-Final-version-1.pdf.

As the 'Health' paper had done, this one too pointed to the link between early unemployment and poor longer-term health and educational outcomes.

After outlining the range of relevant government programmes and schemes then operating, *Outside, Looking In* restated the need to use and increase funding for 'skilled and qualified youth workers', for trained volunteers and for young people to be involved in the design of youth services. These, it said, would help remove barriers to employment, especially if they started 'up-stream' before young people entered training or were actually in work.

### *Young People and the Cost-of-Living Crisis*

With the cost-of-living crisis 'proving ... a deepening challenge' for young people, in March 2023, the NYA launched a 'learning resource ... to assist youth workers and allied professionals ... develop essential money management skills ...' Described as a toolkit, it comprised 12 'independent sessions' covering a range of relevant topics, a variety of games and other resources.[43]

### *Gangs and County Lines Exploitation*

Also in March 2021, the NYA published a paper on gangs' county lines exploitation of young people's 'vulnerabilities' and the role youth workers could play in responding.[44] As, here too, Covid-19 had 'amplified the problem', this again highlighted the '... lack of sufficient youth services and support for young people in many of the county towns and rural areas'. The paper identified a range of consequences of this gap:

- '... an increasing risk to young people from affluent backgrounds ... and (to) girls ... making offending harder to detect'.

[43] NYA 2023, 'Exploring the cost of living crisis resource', March, https://www.nya.org.uk/resource/exploring-the-cost-of-living-crisis/.

[44] NYA, 2021 'Between the lines', March, https://www.nya.org.uk/resource/between-the-lines/#:~:text=A%20new%20report%2C%20Between%20The,young%20people%20across%20county%20lines.

- '… the number of missing vulnerable children (has) soared' so that 'too many children are not identified until exploitation is deeply engrained in their lives'.
- Even as 'children as young as 12 years old are being exploited across county lines …', 'the pandemic has seen a drop in referrals to children's services'.
- '450,000 young people are exposed to risks associated with gangs'.
- 'Around 27,000 children at high risk have not been identified by formal services', resulting in 'too many go(ing) missing between the lines'.

Against this background, the paper concluded, 'the patchwork provision of youth services has left young people … prey to gangs, without a safe space in their communities, among friends with trusted adults and trained youth workers'. As gangs and local dealers changed the way they work, what was required as part of a multi-agency approach was 'the safety-net of open access youth services', to be provided 'in community spaces … supported by detached, street-based youth workers'. This, the paper suggested, should include 'up-skilling and equipping youth workers to maintain contact through social media and online services'.

These proposals were further underpinned by recommendations that included

- 'A high level government strategy for youth workforce development'.
- '… (A) clear (government) plan for detached, outreach and digitalised youth work, with ring-fenced funding'.
- Violence Reduction Units (VRUs) to embed youth services in a public health approach for county lines.
- 'Cross-boundary co-ordination between youth services'.

## The NYA Contribution and Impacts

As a body operating at a distance from its grassroots, the full extent and depth of NYA's impacts are hard to evaluate, not least because much of those 'grass-roots' were small one-night-a-week youth clubs often run by local volunteers. Inevitably, not all of its initiatives anyway will have been greeted with positive bottom-up responses, especially where these sought to push long-established boundaries or challenge more traditional ways of practising and organising.

Nonetheless, as the organisation claiming a leadership role in the 'youth services' arena, NYA clearly sought to make substantial use of its opportunities and its leverage to exert influence at a national level. For open youth work, one potentially less positive example of this (examined critically in Chap. 5) was its contributions to a broadening of the conception of 'youth work' which may have diverted both attention and money from a more strategic government commitment to reinstating the practice's open youth work facilities lost since 2010. Much more positive for those facilities over this period, however, has been the often proactive ways in which NYA has evidenced and analysed what was and what was not happening to them and to young people themselves and its proposed responses.

And all this before account is taken of the key focus of the next chapter—NYA's role over these years in monitoring and extending routes into youth work training and qualifications.

CHAPTER 8

# Training and Qualifications

**Abstract** NYA's 2020 'Functional Map' outlined six 'Functional Areas' of the then-current training structure, process and focuses. After significant falls in course and student numbers (partially recovered by 2023), its 2022 'Youth Workforce Development Strategy to 2027' suggested at least two full-time equivalent qualified youth workers, four youth support workers and trained volunteers in each secondary school catchment area. In its response that year to the government's Youth Guarantee, it also called for the recruitment and training of 10,000 qualified youth workers, 20,000 youth support workers and 40,000 volunteers. After reviewing the National Occupational Standards (NOS), youth work qualifying routes— supported by government-funded bursaries—were extended to include apprenticeships and new degree programmes, with NYA's Academy also offering in-service training opportunities. However, emerging evidence suggested continuing difficulties in filling vacant posts.

**Keywords** Secondary school catchment areas • National Occupational Standards • Training bursaries • Apprenticeships • Degree programmes • In-service training • Job vacancies

## The Role of the NYA

In April 2019, NYA's Chief Executive Leigh Middleton responded to a recently announced government commitment to review youth work qualifications. After a decade of cuts, he pointed particularly to a need for

> ... *boosting the number of youth work degrees, clear pathways for apprenticeships and opening up career opportunities in youth work, from skilled volunteers to advanced professional training.*[1]

These comments indicated what would be key elements of NYA's agenda over this period as, in often proactive ways, it reviewed and further developed training and qualification routes into youth work.

In a paper whose Introduction was dated April 2020,[2] NYA, for example, recorded that

> ... *(it was) updating the Youth Work Curriculum, ... undertak(ing) preliminary work to inform a National Youth Workforce Brief, and ... developing a suite of safeguarding courses for the youth work sector.*

The paper defined the purpose of youth work as

> ... *to facilitate (young people's) personal, social and educational development, to enable them to develop their voice ... and reach their full potential.*

It also explained that in England, the 'relevant associated and emerging policy context' were 'children and young people's services' which, it said, were then 'utilis(ing) youth work for different purposes'. As a result, '... the balance of spend has shifted from being on predominantly universal services to predominantly targeted services', with 'youth workers ... increasingly finding employment in other sectors ...' (see Chap. 5).

Labelling itself 'the Professional Statutory and Regulatory Body for Youth Work in England' (see Chap. 7), in 2022, NYA published a 17-page paper setting out its 'Youth Workforce Development Strategy' to run to

---

[1] Derren Hayes, 2019, 'Youth work reforms need universal focus', *CYPN*, 30 April.

[2] NYA, 2020, *Youth Work in England: Policy, Practice and the National Occupational Standards*, April, https://s3.eu-west-1.amazonaws.com/assets.nya2.joltrouter.net/wp-content/uploads/20210419173602/New-Nos.pdf.

2027.[3] Described as 'intentionally ambitious', it located the Strategy within that wider NYA 'vision' of each secondary school catchment area having at least two full-time equivalent qualified youth workers, at least four youth support workers and trained volunteers (see Chap. 7).

Building on what it called youth work's 'rich and high-quality tradition of training', the Strategy focussed on developing both 'new routes into the profession, and opportunities for workers to develop their knowledge and skills at all points throughout their career'. To help 'encompass the various journeys Youth Workers take', five 'themes' were identified which, the paper said, would 'encourage the growth, development and support of Youth Work across England':

- *Promotion of youth work as a career, and as a methodology*
- *Training and education of practitioners*
- *Links between training organisations and service providers*
- *Developing and supporting sector-specific youth work*
- *Developing infrastructure to support growth and standards*

## THE DECLINE—AND RECOVERY?—OF YOUTH WORK TRAINING

One other key feature of the policy context within which the NYA Strategy had to be implemented was the continuing impact of the post-2010 austerity cuts (see Chap. 3). In a paper published in July 2019, NYA had already noted the conclusion of a recent APPG inquiry into Youth Services—that

> … *traditional training routes of volunteering in a local service … have reduced in number and accessibility, and access to degree level training and management training is also diminished' … Alongside this is an increasing reliance on volunteer workers who … suffer from little recognised available training or on the job support.*[4]

---

[3] NYA, *Youth Workforce Development Strategy 2022–2027*, https://www.nya.org.uk/wp-content/uploads/Public-Workforce-Strategy-Document-final-copy.pdf, accessed 11 July 2023.

[4] NYA, 2019, 'An Update on Routes into Youth Work', 30 July, https://www.nya.org.uk/an-update-on-roures-into-youth-work.

The April 2020 paper referenced above explicitly located the resource pressures then facing youth work training in the two-thirds cut since 2008–09 in local authorities' overall spending on 'Services for Young People'. As a result, it pointed out, in the six years after 2011/12, qualifying training provision in England had declined significantly, with only 41 programmes still operating and by 2017/18 only 432 students enrolled—a drop of over 50 per cent. Other evidence also revealed that the number of full-time JNC-qualified lecturers working on these courses had also fallen steeply.[5]

By 2019–20, NYA's annual report was highlighting that the overall number of students on youth work courses was continuing to fall, with women outnumbering men by three or four to one.[6] Early findings of its ongoing youth work census showed that by September 2022, only 34 per cent of youth work organisations were employing staff with JNC degrees and only 40 per cent with Level 2 qualifications or above.[7]

These losses were illustrated by the contraction of the training programmes of two institutions with a long history of providing—indeed, pioneering—qualifying youth work courses.

- In 2022, Leicester De Montfort University (DMU) announced that it was 'suspending' its youth and community development course whose origins could be traced back to the opening in 1961 of the one-year 'emergency' course recommended by the Albemarle Report.[8]
- Also in 2022, the 135-year-old London YMCA George Williams College—whose distance learning programmes since 2014 had been attracting almost three times the number of students as its full-time course—decided to dismantle its youth work programme and merge with the Centre for Youth Impact (CYI). As the youth work tide turned somewhat (see below), in early 2023, it set out a new long-term strategy. This included commitments to re-launch the College later that year and, by 2026, to re-establish an academic offer focused

[5] Dan Parton, 2019, 'Youth work training figures reveal record lows', *CYPN*, 14 August.

[6] Joe Lepper, 2022, 'Youth work training levels show signs of recovery after hitting record low', *CYPN*, 16 March.

[7] Charlotte Goddard, 2022, Guide to qualifications and training: youth work', *CYPN*, 1 September.

[8] Fiona Simpson, 2022, 'De Montfort University drops youth work and community development course', *CYPN*, 28 July; Ministry of Education, 1960, *The Youth Service in England and Wales*, HMSO, p. 110.

on three 'centres of expertise': 'Youth Impact', 'Quality Practice' and 'Youth Voice'.[9]

However, by March 2022, NYA was confirming that after reaching a record low in 2019–20, four new courses were due to start in the 2020–21 academic year. With another five validated during 2020 and validation discussions in progress on a sixth,[10] by July 2023, 22 institutions were expected to be running 28 youth work programmes. Though recruitment to undergraduate courses had continued to decline slightly, student enrolments overall had by then increased by 10 per cent on the previous year—by 32, to 302—with postgraduate students accounting for 40 per cent of the total. Seventy-nine per cent were women, 46 per cent were people of colour, 20 per cent were disabled and 47 per cent were aged 30 or over.[11]

## TRAINING BURSARIES

In July 2019—that is, well before the NYA's Workforce Development Strategy paper proposed a bursary programme for youth support workers and volunteers—the then youth minister Mims Davies announced £500,000 of government funding for bursaries for youth workers in training. In the context of the wider dismantling of Youth Services since 2010, the initial response from London Youth and other youth sector organisations was, at best, sceptical.[12] Nonetheless, two months later, Davies's successor, Baroness Barran, confirmed the creation of a Youth Worker Bursary Fund to 'provide financial support for 400 people who would otherwise

[9] Tony Jeffs, 2021, 'YMCA and Youth Work Education', *Youth and Policy*, 12 February, https://www.youthandpolicy.org/articles/ymca-youth-work-education/; Fiona Simpson, 2021, 'Centre for Youth Impacts and George Williams College to merge', *CYPN*, 17 November; Fiona Simpson, 2023, 'YMCA College launches five-year youth work strategy', *CYPN*, 27 January.

[10] Joe Lepper, 2022, 'Youth work training levels show signs of recovery after hitting record low', *CYPN*, 16 March.

[11] NYA, 2023, 'HEI Annual Monitoring Survey 2020/2021', https://www.nya.org.uk/hei-annual-monitoring-survey-2023/ 17 July; NYA, 2023, 'Annual Monitoring Report 2020/2021', July, https://s3.eu-west-1.amazonaws.com/assets.nya2.joltrouter.net/wp-content/uploads/2023/07/17114950/HEI-Annual-monitoring-final-2021-2022.pdf; Megan Warren-Lister, 2023, More students enrolling on youth work courses, NYA finds', *CYPN*, 27 July.

[12] Joanne Parkes, 2019, 'Youth work bursaries dwarfed by scale of cuts, says charity', *CYPN*, 29 July.

not be able to afford to access the approved level 2 and level 3 youth work' qualifications.[13]

Over the next three years, a series of announcements extended the bursaries' offer. When the DCMS published the summary findings of its Youth Review in February 2022 (see Chap. 9), it, for example, confirmed:

> *To encourage people to enter the profession, we will fund approximately 550 bursaries for entry level qualifications in youth work, and continue supporting NYA to produce free online non-accredited learning for anyone working with young people.*[14]

A month later, the NYA announced bursaries funded by £790,000 of government 'investment' in order to increase access to Levels 2 and 3 qualifications for 547 workers in 'under-represented' parts of the youth sector.[15] A further 500 bursaries were confirmed in February 2023 specifically to encourage young people to train as youth workers, with some 570 placements to be made available for Level 2 and 3 qualifications and 130 for what was then a new Level 4 'certificate in professional development'.[16]

## An Academy for Youth Work

Another key feature of NYA's work over these years was the promotion of a range of in-service training opportunities, many of which after March 2019 could be accessed through its newly launched Youth Work Academy.[17] Described as 'a collaborative learning space dedicated to training and development in the youth work sector', the Academy's stated aim was to

---

[13] GOV.UK, 2019, 'Hundreds of students to take youth work qualifications after new government investment', 12 September, https://www.gov.uk/government/news/hundreds-of-students-to-take-youth-work-qualifications-after-new-government-investment; Joe Lepper, 2019, 'Government announces details of bursary for disadvantaged youth work students', *CYPN*, 12 September.

[14] GOV.UK, 2022, *Youth Review: Summary findings and government response*, 1 February, p. 9.

[15] Fiona Simpson, 2022, 'NYA launches new round of training bursaries', *CYPN*, 9 March.

[16] Emily Harle, 2023, 'NYA launches hundreds of free youth work training places' *CYPN*, 8 February.

[17] Joe Lepper, 2019, 'Youth work academy launches with training to tackle gang crime', *CYPN*, 14 March; NYA, 'The NYA Youth Work Academy', https://www.nya.org.uk/skills/academy/, accessed 20 June 2023; Charlotte Goddard, 2022, Guide to qualifications and training: youth work', *CYPN*, 1 September.

'... enhance the skills of Youth Work practitioners through our dedicated online learning platform by providing post-qualifying training opportunities ...'. These were to include both NYA's own virtual and face-to-face courses and what it called 'a catalogue of courses from across the sector'.[18]
Examples of how this commitment was implemented included:[19]

- A selection of 12 free 'virtual' continuing professional development courses, announced in August 2021.[20]
- Monthly online 'tea breaks' and 'supper breaks', with the former explained as '... a reflective platform to enable practitioners to come together and explore common themes which impact our practice on a daily basis ... (and) engage in critical thinking and dialogue'.[21]
- Partnership with the Equal Equity project in a programme to 'capacity build Black and practitioners of colour into Leadership, Management and Policy'. This ran a first national 'Power of Now' conference in Leicester in 2022 entitled Racial Justice and Youth Work.[22]
- A first session on 'Child Criminal Exploitation, Violence and County Lines', with (by mid-2023) courses planned on detached youth work, using cognitive behavioural therapy, meeting young people's mental health needs, the effects of social media on their lives and improving their financial skills.[23]

The Academy also offered 'bespoke training' on 'a range of professional development needs, from those new to youth work to qualified

[18] Charlotte Goddard, 2022, Guide to qualifications and training: youth work', *CYPN*, 1 September.

[19] Joe Lepper, 2019, 'Youth work academy launches with training to tackle gang crime', *CYPN*, 14 March; Charlotte Goddard, 2020, 'Youth work – children's workforce guide to qualifications and training', *CYPN*, 29 September.

[20] NYA, 2021, 'NYA, 'Youth Work Academy launch a new suite of free CDP opportunities', 11 August, https://www.nya.org.uk/nya-youth-work-academy-launch-a-new-suite-of-free-cpd-opportunities/.

[21] NYA, 'NYA Events', https://www.nya.org.uk/skills/live-programmes/nya-events/ accessed 7 July 2023.

[22] NYA, 'Equal Equity Impact Incubator: What is Equal Equity?', https://www.nya.org.uk/skills/live-programmes/equal-equity/, accessed 13 July 2023.

[23] Joe Lepper, 2019, 'Youth work academy lunches with training to tackle gang crime', *CYPN*, 14 March; NYA, https://www.nya.org.uk/nya-youth-work-academy-launches/ accessed 9 July 2023.

practitioners who are developing their practice and competencies'. With 'each of our courses … developed by subject experts, ensuring content is of the highest quality for learners', NYA presented its offer as '… online digital blended learning (which) fits the needs of both organisations and youth workers, providing learners with global access to sector experts'.[24]

To support youth workers at the height of the Covid outbreak, NYA also collaborated with UK Youth to create a website offering training and other resources, including a digital introduction to detached youth work.[25]

## ROUTES TO YOUTH WORK QUALIFICATIONS

### *Reviewing and Revising the National Occupational Standards*

As a number of its papers made clear, an essential starting point for one of NYA's highest priorities—reviewing and extending the routes to initial training and qualification—was the National Occupational Standards (NOS). These had been defined as

> … *recognised by employers as the clear, concise and consistent articulation of requirements for occupational competence and the knowledge and skills individuals need to develop to perform effectively and safely in the workplace.*[26]

After a consultation and review process carried out partly in collaboration with the APPG inquiry into Youth Services, in February 2019, NYA released its own revised version of the NOS which, in a follow-up paper in July, it described as '… vital for, and supported by, the sector'.[27] With a message from the joint chairs of its Education Training Standards (ETS) Committee dated April 2020, the initial version of its paper *Youth Work in*

[24] NYA, 'The NYA Youth Work Academy', https://www.nya.org.uk/skills/academy/ accessed 5 July 2023.
[25] Charlotte Goddard, 2020, 'Youth work – children's workforce guide to qualifications and training', *CYPN*, 29 September.
[26] UK Commission for Employment and Skills, 2010, *NOS Strategy 2010–2020*, https://assets.publishing.service.gov.uk/government/uploads/system/uploads/attachment_data/file/304235/nos-strategy-2011.pdf.
[27] *NOS Consultation: Updated Functional Map*, 2019, February, https://cldstandardscouncil.org.uk/wp-content/uploads/NOSFunctionalMap.pdf; NYA, 2019, 'An Update on Routes into Youth Work', 30 July, https://www.nya.org.uk/an-update-on-roures-into-youth-work.

*England*[28] also emphasised that the standards '... have always underpinned ... the Youth Work Curriculum'—to which by then both NYA and the DCMS were giving renewed attention (see Chaps. 4 and 7). The paper argued that the standards 'provide core competencies across the whole spectrum of JNC recognised training in England' and that therefore they were relevant to all available or planned youth work qualifying routes. Including a 120-page Appendix, it then set out how they related to youth work using a 'Functional Map' and tables outlining six 'Functional Areas' of the current training structure, process and focuses.[29]

### *Extending Training and Qualifying Routes into Youth Work*

Within the overall NOS framework, NYA continued to review and extend the sector's initial full- and part-time training and qualifications routes—a commitment which in 2019 included its ETS Committee working with employers, unions, universities and others to establish flexible routes to qualification.[30] Though later revised,[31] the paper published in April 2020 summarised these routes as 'Initial Youth Work Qualifications ...', 'Professionally validated degree programmes' and 'Current and proposed apprenticeships for youth work at both Level 3 and Level 6'.[32]

Intended to offer joined-up 'pathways ... for structured youth work training for all ...', approval of the Level 3 apprenticeship was announced in September 2020.[33] That month, in collaboration with awarding bodies and the sector more widely, NYA also completed a review of Level 2 and 3 qualifications. According to its Director of Youth Work, this had resulted in a 'new, modernised suite of qualifications reflect(ing) the contemporary

---

[28] NYA, 2020, *Youth Work in England: Policy, Practice and the National Occupational Standards*, May, https://s3.eu-west-1.amazonaws.com/assets.nya2.joltrouter.net/wp-content/uploads/20210419173602/New-Nos.pdf.

[29] NYA, 2020, *Youth Work in England*.

[30] NYA, 2019, 'An Update on Routes into Youth Work', 30 July, https://www.nya.org.uk/an-update-on-routes-into-youth-work/.

[31] See NOS, 'News Updates', https://www.ukstandards.org.uk/en/news, accessed 25 June 2023.

[32] NYA, 2020, *Youth Work in England*.

[33] NYA, 2020, 'Level 3 Youth Support Worker Apprenticeship Approved', 28 September, https://www.nya.org.uk/level-3-youth-support-worker-apprentivceship-approved/, accessed 16 July 2023.

needs of young people, such as a unit related to trauma-informed practice, and another on gangs and youth violence'.[34]

Two years later, a 'Guide to Youth Work',[35] published by the *Children and Young People Now* (*CYPN*) magazine in association with the NYA, provided fuller definitions of the available routes.

- An apprenticeship was an opportunity '… for young people and adult learners to earn while they learn in a real job'.
- A Level 2 or 3 certificate or diploma in Youth Work Practice was for workers in a youth support worker role.
- The Professional Youth Worker role was for workers who have passed a JNC-recognised youth work degree course which 'confer(s) the status of qualified youth worker'.

By the time it appeared, the Guide was also stressing that these trained youth workers were even more needed given the '… challenges to young people, from the socio-economic impact of the pandemic, to reductions in service provision and severely impacted educational opportunities'.

By the time the Level 6 'Degree Youth Work Apprenticeship' was approved (in September 2021), NYA was working with university partners and the Institute for Apprenticeships and Technical Education to create a funding band—approved by January 2022.[36] This was followed a year later by the launch of a Level 4 'Certificate in Professional Development (Youth Work)'—described by NYA as reflecting its five-year Workforce Development Strategy[37] and, in July 2023, by an announcement of the

---

[34] Charlotte Goddard, 2020, 'Youth work – children's workforce guide to qualifications and training', *CYPN*, 29 September.

[35] NYA, 2022, 'Guide to Youth Work', *CYPN*, 8 March, https://www.cypnow.co.uk/features/article/guide-to-youth-work; https://flickread.com/edition/html/free/6225f0ce591f0#1.

[36] NYA, 2021, 'New Level 6 Degree Youth Work Apprenticeship approved', September, https://www.nya.org.uk/new-level-6-degree-youth-work-apprenticeship%E2%80%AFapproved/.

[37] NYA, 2023, 'New qualification for youth work professionals to build skills of the sector', 12 January, https://www.nya.org.uk/new-qualification-for-youth-work-professionals-to-build-skills-of-sector/, Fiona Simpson, 2023, 'NYA launches new youth work qualification', *CYPN*, 13 January.

planned launch of a Level 2 qualification in youth work practice which would allow students to study flexibly within a 6–12-month timescale.[38]

By mid-2023, NYA was reporting that to meet a growing demand for qualified youth workers, sector leaders were calling for the apprenticeship routes to qualification to be enhanced across the country. These were seen as particularly valuable for 'mature' students able to bring broader life experience to their learning as well, often, as substantial previous practice experience. However, anecdotal evidence also began to emerge that the educational establishments and field-based organisations implementing the apprenticeship routes were having to negotiate bureaucratic and practical problems such as a mismatch between a 30-hours-a-week apprenticeship contract and part-time youth worker posts of often only 18 hours a week.

In March 2024, the NYA website was listing the following routes to a youth worker qualification:[39]

*Level 2 Award in Youth Work Principles*
Not JNC approved.
An introductory accredited youth work qualification

*Level 2 Certificate in Youth Work Practice*
JNC approved at Youth Support Worker Level
Designed for people already working or volunteering in a youth work setting.

*Level 3 Diploma in Youth Work Practice (Apprenticeship)*
JNC approved at Youth Support Worker Level.
Taken while working in a youth work setting.

*Level 3 Certificate in Youth Work Practice*
JNC approved at Youth Support Worker Level
Requires evidence of involvement in a 20-hour youth work project.

*Level 3 Diploma in Youth Work Practice*
JNC approved at Youth Support Worker Level
Includes an 80 hours placement in a youth work environment

[38] Megan Warren-Lister, 2023, More students enrolling on youth work courses, NYA finds', *CYPN*, 27 July.
[39] NYA, 'Becoming a youth worker', https://www.nya.org.uk/becoming-a-youth-worker/#accordion-available-qualifications, accessed 19 February 2024.

*BA (Hons) or BSc (Hons)*
JNC approved at Professional Youth Worker Level
To support career development for those already working (either paid or unpaid).

*Level 6 Integrated Degree*
JNC approved at Professional Youth Worker Level
For people employed for at least 30 hours a week in a youth work setting.

*Postgraduate Diploma, MA or MSc*
JNC approved at Professional Youth Worker Level
Designed for graduates already working in a relevant employment setting (either paid or unpaid) to allow further progress in their professional development.

The NYA website also gave links to ten higher education institutions and two theological colleges in England which, also in February 2024, were providing approved routes to professional youth work qualifications.[40]

## Into the Future

In late 2022, NYA responded to the government's recently announced Youth Guarantee by calling for the recruitment and training of 10,000 qualified youth workers, 20,000 youth support workers and 40,000 volunteers (see Chap. 7). However, Kevin Jones, the head of NYA's workforce and professional development, assumed that these workers 'were likely to find themselves working in a school, providing mental health support, … running adventure activities, or based in a hospital or even inside a prison'[41] (see Chap. 5). Less clear, therefore—even uncertain—was how far the NYA efforts in this period to extend and diversify youth work's training and qualifying routes specifically benefited open youth work.

However, acknowledged in passing by Jones in his paper was a deeper systemic problem which was also impeding the practice's potential gains

[40] NYA, 'Becoming a Youth Worker: Available Qualifications', https://www.nya.org.uk/becoming-a-youth-worker/, accessed March 2024.
[41] Kevin Jones, 2022, 'Guide to Youth Work: Youth Work Developments', *CYPN*, 8 March.

from the NYA qualification initiatives: the serious shortage of applicants for both full-time and part-time posts, especially from people with some previous experience of the practice.[42]

A key causal factor here was clearly those deep post-2010 cuts to local Youth Services which had resulted both in the huge exodus of professional and skilled staff and in the sharp fall in the number of students enrolling on qualifying courses. However, though the evidence is again often only anecdotal, another more deeply embedded problem may also have been at work here, largely unrecognised at the policy level: that in the past a—perhaps even the—main route into 'professional' youth work for many people had been via their previous involvement in those lost youth work facilities. Though individuals could, of course, have very different experiences and much might depend on the on-the-job support and training they received, the key stages had been: becoming a youth club member; moving as an older teenager into what was often called a 'senior member' role; opting later to train as a 'voluntary helper' or part-time paid worker; followed, albeit by a small number, by a decision to qualify as a 'professional' youth worker.[43]

From 2010 onwards—including in the residential field[44]—opportunities such as these reduced significantly and, in many areas, disappeared altogether. With them too, therefore, went a crucial experiential route and process for people to understand first-hand what open youth work involved and required, to internalise its distinctive ways of working—and, with that as a key part of the motivation, to make it their career choice.

[42] Emily Harle, 2023, 'Youth organisations face changing landscape of residential schemes', *CYPN*, 30 August.

[43] John Holmes, *Professionalisation – a misleading myth? A study of the careers of ex-students of youth and community work courses in England and Wales from 1970 to 1978*, National Youth Bureau, 1981, pp. 37, 40.

[44] Emily Harle, 2023, 'Youth organisations face a changing landscape of residential schemes', *CYPN*, 30 August.

# CHAPTER 9

# The National Policy Contexts

**Abstract** An NYA paper published in 2020 concluded that 'there is currently no explicit statement for what the English Government intends youth work to achieve'. Over the period covered by this book, this gap was partially filled by a review of its statutory guidance to local authorities; its '… ambitious, long-term £500 million (Youth Investment Fund) plan …' often linked to its 'levelling-up agenda'; and a DCMS-led 'Youth Review'. The latter brought responses from young people, academics and the DCMS itself and generated the announcement of a National Youth Guarantee. At no point, however, did the government commit itself to fully and systematically reinstating the open youth work facilities lost after 2010.

**Keywords** Statutory guidance • Youth Investment Fund • Levelling up • Youth Review • National Youth Guarantee

## Where Are the Youth Policies?

Though focused primarily on training and qualifications (see Chap. 8), the NYA paper published in April 2020 made a number of critical comments on the government's failure to give consistent and dedicated attention to

B. Davies, *Youth Work Policies in England 2019–2023*,
https://doi.org/10.1007/978-3-031-65636-1_9

youth work and its provision nationally.[1] It, for example, suggested that, with 'local authorities ... utilis(ing) youth work for different purposes', 'there is currently no explicit statement for what the English Government intends youth work to achieve and no National Youth Work strategy'. While acknowledging that the statutory guidance for local authorities was being reviewed (see below), the paper also noted that

> ... at present, there is no indication as to what levels of youth work should be delivered or how, nor what types of youth work activities should be undertaken or what it should aim to achieve.

As the Covid impacts on young people became clear, a *CYPN* article by the then Youth Minister Baroness Barron published in August 2020 sought to reassure readers that the government was acting to fill these gaps.[2] With a strong emphasis on 'listening carefully to young people' and 'allow(ing) them to contribute to "building back better"', it highlighted the Education Department's £1 billion Covid catch-up fund, the £2 billion Kickstart Scheme to help 16–24-year-olds into jobs and—most relevant to youth workers—the YIF's '... ambitious, long-term £500 million plan for youth services' (see Chap. 3).

However, the departure two years later of her successor Nigel Huddleston, followed within a month by the resignation of *his* successor Lord Kammal, raised questions about the role of Youth Minister and whether this should remain part of a DCMS brief that at the time also included sport, heritage and tourism.[3] By the time Secretary of State Lucy Frazer presented her department's vision for the youth sector in a speech to the centre-right think tank Onward in July 2023, the DCMS website was making no reference to a youth minister role.[4] Two months later, Frazer was also making it clear that 'youth work is not the responsibility of

[1] NYA, 2020, 'Youth Work in England: Policy, Practice and the National Occupational Standards', May, https://s3.eu-west-1.amazonaws.com/assets.nya2.joltrouter.net/wp-content/uploads/20210419173602/New-Nos.pdf.

[2] Baroness Barron, 2020, 'Youth Minister: Young people have a key role to play in nation's recovery', *CYPN*, 12 August.

[3] Joe Lepper, 2022, 'Future of youth minister role undecided following Huddleston's departure, *CYPN*, 22 September; Fiona Simpson, 2022, 'Lord Kamall confirmed as youth mister', *CYPN*, 26 September.

[4] GOV.UK, 2023, 'Lucy Frazer's speech at the Onward Think Tank', 19 July, https://www.gov.uk/government/speeches/lucy-frazers-speech-at-the-onward-think-tank.

just one department' (i.e. the DCMS) and that in particular 'the Department for Education is responsible for education and that's had record funding'.[5]

## STATUTORY GUIDANCE

One significant commitment the government did make in this period, in July 2019,[6] was to strengthen its statutory guidance to local authorities on their duty to provide 'youth services', including open youth work.[7] According to the minister at the time, the aim was to focus on the 'positive role local authorities can play in securing and offering services to young people' and 'provide greater clarity on government's expectations of them'.[8]

Dating back at least to the 1944 Education Act and last updated in 2012, the guidance had over the years often proved ineffective and even confusing. This, not least, was because, rather than actually naming youth work—or even, as it was called in the 1944 Act, 'youth leadership'—it talked only of local authority provision of '... adequate facilities for ... leisure-time occupation ... and recreative activities ... for persons over compulsory school age'.[9]

Despite a number of revisions over the years,[10] a survey in 2014 had revealed that in local authorities' decisions on youth services' funding, the guidance was playing a role 'all of the time' in only 41 of 97 local authorities.[11] Even when it was applied, the fact that it allowed these services to be 'secured' only 'so far as is reasonably practicable' had given

---

[5] Fiona Simpson, 2023, 'Youth services is a cross-government responsibility, say Culture Secretary', *CYPN*, 28 September.

[6] GOV.UK, 2019, 'Review launched into statutory guidance for Local Authorities on providing youth services', 10 July, https://www.gov.uk/government/news/review-launched-into-statutory-guidance-for-local-authorities-on-providing-youth-services.

[7] Derren Hayes, 2023, 'Access to Youth Work: Special Report', *CYPN*, 24 October.

[8] Joanne Parkes, 2019, 'Government launches review of youth work guidance', *CYPN*, 10 July.

[9] See Bernard Davies, 1999, *From Voluntaryism to the Welfare State: A History of the Youth Service in England Volume 1 1939–1979*, Youth Work Press, pp. 22–24.

[10] DCSF, 2008, *Statutory Guidance on Chapter 507B Education Act 1996*, DCFS, March, para 19, DfES, (2007) 'Statutory Guidance on Chapter 6 of Education and Inspections Act'.

[11] Laura McCardle, 2014, '"Youth minister Rob Wilson rejects statutory services motion"', *CYPN*, 4 December.

many councils a 'get-out' rationale, especially when they needed to cut budgets.[12] The call for public evidence—initially due to start in August 2019, then delayed until October[13]—quickly prompted demands from the field for fundamental changes to the guidance, with many of the critical responses focused on the 'reasonably practicable' clause.[14]

As outlined in Chap. 7, the NYA both contributed to and supported the guidance review process. Its ETS Sub-Committee, for example, planned to 'dovetail' the development of its Youth Work Strategy with this.[15] It also very explicitly addressed the 'reasonably practicable' ambiguities with its proposals that, to ensure 'quality and sufficiency', each secondary school catchment area should have at least two full-time equivalent JNC-qualified youth workers, at least four youth support workers and trained volunteers.[16]

Further delayed by the Covid pandemic,[17] an updated guidance document was finally released in September 2023.[18] With a focus now on '… improv(ing) young people's well being', this required local authorities to make a 'youth offer' to 13–19-year-olds and to 20–24-year-olds with learning difficulties or disabilities. As well as providing opportunities for them to reach their full potential, the offer was also intended to

[12] See, for example, Department for Education, 2012, *Consultation on Draft Revised Statutory Guidance for Local Authorities on Services and Activities to Improve Young People's Wellbeing*, 5 March; Laura McCardle, 2014, 'Youth funding and services cut as councils overlook legal duty', *CYPN*, 22 July.

[13] Joanne Parkes, 2019, 'Government launches review of youth work guidance', *CYPN*, 10 July; Derren Hayes, 2019, 'Call for evidence into council youth work duties', *CYPN*, 3 October.

[14] Derren Hayes, 2020, 'Statutory guidance Review: youth bodies set out the case for change', *CYPN*, 2 January.

[15] Charlotte Goddard, 2020, 'Youth work – Children's Workforce Guide to Qualifications and Training' *CYPN*, 29 September.

[16] NYA, 2020, 'Guidance for Local Authorities on Providing Youth Services', p. 4, October, https://static.nya.org.uk/static/ee06e7a621f49e562f71119d5fe524ac/The-Role-and-Sufficiency-of-Youth-Services-V06.pdf.

[17] Fiona Simpson, 2021, 'Youth Service statutory guidance review delayed by Covid-19', *CYPN*, 5 February.

[18] GOV.UK, 2023, 'Statutory guidance for local authorities on services to improve young people's well being', https://www.gov.uk/government/publications/statutory-guidance-for-local-authorities-youth-provision/statutory-guidance-for-local-authorities-on-services-to-improve-young-peoples-well-being, 23 September.

*… make an important contribution to other objectives, such as economic, social and environmental improvements, community cohesion, safer and stronger neighbourhoods, better health and increased educational attainment and employment.*

Proposed ways for achieving these objectives included local authorities ensuring 'the right mix of open access services and targeted services' and the introduction of 'digital offers'. They were also required to 'consult and take into account the views of young people in their area'—especially those 'facing particular barriers to accessing sufficient provision, such as disadvantaged young people and vulnerable young people'. However, not only did the document twice confirm the 'so far as reasonably practicable' clause, including in its 68-word 'Overview', but it also allowed application of the guidance to '… depend on the specific circumstances of the local authority and the particular requirements for access to such activities and facilities'.

As noted in Chap. 3, the LGA was prompted by the new guidance to call for the Chancellor's Autumn Statement to include additional funding for youth work—a plea which, though ignored in the Statement, the DCMS later claimed was being met by, for example, money allocated from its Million Hour Fund (see below). A different but no less telling question about the new guidance was posed by James Cathcart, the Director of Young Voices Heard: 'who will be checking whether (its) "musts" are delivered this time around?'[19] And, though acknowledging that the guidance did bring some greater clarity to councils' responsibilities, Leigh Middleton, the Chief Executive of NYA, announced that the Agency would be offering a tool to support them to '… take the necessary steps to ensure that their provision meets local need, legislation and is effective'[20] (see Chap. 7).

---

[19] Fiona Simpson, 2023, 'Sector hopes updated sufficiency rules will boost access to youth services' *CYPN*, 24 October.

[20] NYA, 2023, 'How to fulfil your Statutory Duty under Section 507B of the Education Act: A toolkit for local authorities', undated, accessed 1 December 2023, https://s3.eu-west-1.amazonaws.com/assets.nya2.joltrouter.net/wp-content/uploads/2023/09/29102527/NYA_How-to-fulfil-your-Statutory-Duty-A-toolkit-for-local-authorities-1.pdf.

## ANOTHER 'YOUTH REVIEW'

Three years before the new guidance appeared the government had embarked on a much more ambitious youth work-focused initiative when, as part of its December 2020 Spending Review, the Treasury announced a DCMS-led 'youth review'.[21] Its stated purpose was, to 2025, to '... outlin(e) a clear direction for the out-of-school youth agenda, including considering the next steps on the Youth Investment Fund and the NCS programme'. Its overall aims included to '... ensure that longer-term spending and programmes achieve ... **level-up opportunity** across the country' by addressing regional differences such as—as Baroness Barron put it—'Why where you live determines the access you have'. The DCMS—again reflecting some continuing neo-liberal concerns—also stressed the need 'to develop (young people's) **skills for work and life**' and 'to support **mental and physical health and wellbeing**' (emphases in the original).

In collaboration with the NYA's National Youth Sector Advisory Board, providers, 'representative groups' (which included academics) and young people were invited to respond to the Review via two digital questionnaires.[22] Responses were received from some 6000 young people aged 11–18, from over 170 youth sector organisations, from 32 academics/ researchers and from other government departments.[23]

Though the concluding date for the Review had been set originally for May 2021, the DCMS's report was not released until February 2022.[24]

---

[21] NYA, 2021, 'Treasury rapid review of government youth policies', 11 February, https://www.nya.org.uk/treasury-rapid-review-of-government-youth-policies/.

[22] NYA, 2021, 'Treasury rapid review of government youth policies', 11 February, https://www.nya.org.uk/treasury-rapid-review-of-government-youth-policies/; GOV.UK, 2021, 'Youth Sector Engagement Exercise', DCMS, 2021, 23 February, https://www.gov.uk/government/publications/engagement-exercise-on-out-of-school-support-for-young-people/youth-sector-engagement-exercise; Derren Hayes, 2021, 'Youth Policy and funding review', *CYPN*, 23 February.

[23] PALYCW Members' Bulletin, 2021, 'DCMS Spring Review and The Association's Consultation response', 30 April.

[24] DCMS, 2022, *Youth Review: Summary findings and government response*, 1 February, 'Ministerial foreword', pp. 3, 8, https://www.gov.uk/government/publications/youth-review-summary-findings-and-government-response/youth-review-summary-findings-and-government-response.

## RESPONSES TO THE REVIEW

### *From Young People …*

From a youth work perspective, some of the Review's most significant findings clarified what young people saw as most valuable about their involvement in 'youth services and youth clubs'. This was summarised as:

- *Having something fun to do after school/in the holidays/on weekends*
- *Making new friends*
- *Learning new skills*
- *Having a place to go for young people outside of school*
- *Being able to meet people from different backgrounds and mix with different cultures*
- *Having a place where I can be myself*
- *Being able to participate in lots of different activities*
- *Social interaction and coming together to create something*

As much as they had appreciated how '… the youth sector had adapted to keep supporting them during the pandemic', they also were clear that for them digital methods 'did not replace the need for in person opportunities'.[25]

Young people also fed back on the 'barriers' they experienced to their involvement in open youth work facilities. Here, as well as highlighting the 'loss of youth provision … due to funding cuts', they talked specifically of the 'quality of provision'. For them, the Review found, this was defined in part by opportunities to meet 'trained and passionate youth workers or volunteers' who would 'create an inclusive and welcoming environment, where young people felt supported and respected'.[26]

### *… From the Academics …*

As well as highlighting the need for 'positive evidence around the impact of youth services', the academics who responded stressed the importance of providing accessible and long-term funding for 'universal services'. In particular, they proposed that 'where capital funding was needed it should

[25] DCMS, 2022, *Youth Review*, p. 6.
[26] DCMS, 2022, *Youth Review*, p 6.

be small-scale, flexible and locally determined' so that it was available for what they called 'pop-up or modular builds'[27]—a perspective which, as argued in Chap. 6, contrasted sharply with that driving the creation across the country of multi-million-pound, town-centre OnSide Youth Zones.

### … And from the DCMS

In its Introduction to the report, the DCMS explained its own overall aspirations as to 'provide young people with somewhere to go, something to do and someone to talk to …' and to give them 'the opportunity to build a relationship with a trusted adult'. It particularly noted the 'significant role' this provision played for an estimated 450,000 young people '… not yet known to statutory services'.[28]

More specifically, it said it would develop a Youth Sector Strategy to '… provide clarity on the government's role in supporting youth services', to be implemented through a new National Youth Guarantee backed by some of the £560 million allocated to the YIF. With the DCMS taking the lead 'in enabling effective youth participation in decision-making at all levels', the Guarantee confirmed the 'up to 300 new and refurbished youth spaces and services for the country's most left behind areas' so that 'by 2025 every young person in England will have access to regular clubs and activities, adventures away from home and volunteering opportunities'.[29]

Eighteen months later, Frazer explained in more detail how the funding allocated to implement the Guarantee was being used.[30] This included:

- £19 million of (not government but Lottery) money from the Million Hour Fund to 'help tackle anti-social behaviour and improve access to opportunities such as cooking lessons, day trips and sporting activities during the summer holidays'.
- £1.5 million bursary funding for up to 7500 'disadvantaged' young people to access 'adventures away from home'.

[27] DCMS, 2022, *Youth Review*, p. 7.
[28] DCMS, 2022, *Youth Review*, p. 5.
[29] DCMS, 2022, *Youth Review*, pp. 3, 8.
[30] GOV.UK, 2023, 'Millions awarded to youth services for summer activities', 28 August, https://www.gov.uk/government/news/millions-awarded-to-youth-services-for-summer-holiday-activities; Fiona Simpson, 2023, 'Youth services is a cross-government responsibility, say Culture Secretary', *CYPN*, 28 September.

- £300,000 to improve eight regional youth work units' co-ordination of services.
- £250,000 to encourage local partnerships.

This money may have contributed to the 4 per cent rise between 2021 and 2022 in both the total and the per-head council spending on young people's services, recorded by the YMCA in October 2023. However, as the YMCA report also made clear, it fell a long way short of reinstating the around 75 per cent cut in that spending over the previous decade—from £1.46 billion to £377 million.[31]

The Youth Review Report also promised that within government more widely as well as across its own department, the DCMS would seek 'greater alignment … to maximise and coordinate funding opportunities for the youth sector'.[32] This came with the commitment of the £790,000 allocation in 2022–23 to create 547 bursaries to support workers doing Level 2 and 3 youth work training (see Chap. 8) and with a proposal—first indicated in September 2020 by the Institute for Youth Work[33]—to 'for the first time set up a National Youth Work Register to bolster the professional standing of youth work …'

When probed further, however, the DCMS's responses to the Review left some key issues unresolved. Some—explored in Chap. 3—were concerned with the funding for the Youth Guarantee and its channelling through the YIF. Others (discussed above) related the statutory guidance to local authorities on which, in one 30-word sentence—and nine months after its original promised launch date—the Review report merely confirmed an intention to 'conduct a review'.[34]

As some of the quotes above indicate, the Youth Review Report also repeatedly located its youth work proposals in the government's wider 'levelling up agenda'.[35] In her Foreword, the DCMS Secretary of State at the time, Nadine Dorries, talked, for example, of her Department's commitment 'to ensuring all young people are given opportunities, levelling up where they are under-served, socially excluded and economically

---

[31] Derren Hayes, 2023, 'Access to Youth Work: Key policy developments', *CYPN*, 24 October.

[32] DCMS, 2022, *Youth Review*, p. 9.

[33] Charlotte Goddard, 2020, 'Youth work – children's workforce guide to qualifications and training', *CYPN*, 29 September.

[34] DCMS, 2022, *Youth Review*, p. 9.

[35] DCMS, 2022, *Youth Review*, pp. 3, 8–9.

disadvantaged'. Both her Foreword to the Review and the report itself carried promises to 'ensure that our spending and programmes meet the needs of young people as well as our ambitions on "levelling up"'; and that the Youth Guarantee would have a firm focus on this. Two sub-sections of the Report had 'levelling up' in their titles, with one promising specifically that the 300 new and expanded youth centres would be for '... levelling up youth infrastructure in "left-behind" places, so young people who are most in need have access to youth workers and positive activities'.

All this, however, has to be placed in the context of some of the government's wider statements and actions over these years. In 2023, for example, in her speeches and statement as the DCMS Culture Secretary at the time, Lucy Frazer explicitly explained her 'passions and priorities' for supporting young people, not as open youth work's informal educational practice, but as

> *... preventative work, in order to make sure they don't go down the wrong path, it helps them to get into employment, it makes sure that they have good wellbeing and good physical health.*[36]

For achieving these aspirations, she particularly looked to 'guide leaders, sports team coaches (and) music teachers' and to young people joining 'scouts, guides, and tak(ing) part in the DoE scheme'.[37]

Similar expectations emerged from the 'Levelling up' White Paper published in the same month as the Youth Review Report (February 2022). In its 16-page Executive Summary, one of just two comments on young people and 'youth services' reinforced the 'they're-up-to-no-good' youth stereotype by promising '... to make sure 16- and 17-year olds who commit crimes pay their community back with visible labour to improve the local environment'. The other—buried in a 135-word paragraph on page 15 to which the DCMS Youth Review Report made no reference— repeated the Youth Guarantee commitments to all young people having access to 'out of school activities, adventures away from home and

---

[36] Fiona Simpson, 2023, 'Youth services is a cross-government responsibility, say Culture Secretary', *CYPN*, 28 September.

[37] GOV.UK, 2023, 'Lucy Frazer's speech at the Onward Thin Tank', 19 July, https://www.gov.uk/government/speeches/lucy-frazers-speech-at-the-onward-think-tank.

opportunities to volunteer', including by embedding the DoE Award Scheme in every secondary school.[38]

However, perhaps particularly revealing of what, for the governments of this period, was high priority 'youth work' was this paragraph's last two sentences:

> *We will give more students the transformative opportunity to join the cadets, providing more support to the state school sector to* ***increase Combined Cadet Force participation***. (Emphasis in the original). *This will include linking funding of cadet units in private schools with a requirement to ensure support for the expansion of cadet forces in state schools and open access to nearby state school students.*[39]

[38] HM Government, 2022 'Levelling up in the United Kingdom: Executive Summary', February, p. 15, https://assets.publishing.service.gov.uk/government/uploads/system/uploads/attachment_data/file/1052046/Executive_Summary.pdf.

[39] HM Government, 2022, 'Levelling up in the United Kingdom: Executive Summary', p. 15.

# Epilogue: June 2024

## Can Open Youth Work Survive—And If So How?

As highlighted in previous chapters, a crucial policy context for the youth work developments analysed in this book has been the deep and embedded reservations of the Conservative governments of the period about public services and their financing. Though clearly a strong motivation here has been to cut government expenditure, often substantially, the policy has also been driven ideologically by the conviction that, in principle, the role and reach of the state needs to be cut back.

Not only, therefore, has that assault on public services been ongoing throughout the period covered by this book[1] but overall it seems likely to continue. With the Conservatives giving the highest profile to introducing compulsory national service for young people, only the Labour Party's 2024 general election manifesto mentioned anything coming close to

---

[1] Melanie May, 2024, 'Two-fifths of charities using reserves and asking funder for more help as need and costs soar', UK Fundraising, 19 January, https://fundraising.co.uk/2024/01/19/two-fifths-of-charities-using-reserves-asking-funders-for-more-help-as-need-costs-soar/#:~:text=soar%20%2D%20UK%20Fundraising-,Two%2Dfifths%20of%20charities%20using%20reserves%20%26%20asking%20funders%20for%20more,help%20as%20need%20%26%20costs%20soar&text=Soaring%20need%20for%20charities'%20services,reserves%20to%20meet%20operational%20costs; Patrick Butler, 2024, 'Charities warn of "devastating knock-on impact" of English councils' financial crisis' *Guardian*, 3 February.

youth work or even to youth services more broadly. Though its launch by Keir Starmer was greeted by a protesters' banner proclaiming 'Youth Deserve Better', it, for example, promised £20 million to help place youth workers in A&E departments and—to prevent young people from being drawn into crime—£95 million for a network of 'youth hubs' and local 'prevention partnerships' also partly staffed by youth workers.[2] Indeed, despite warnings from the International Monetary Fund,[3] a government desperate to avoid election annihilation continued to prioritise tax cuts over investment in public services while a Labour government-in-waiting seemed to be suggesting that it, too, would in effect opt for a renewed version of austerity.

The question posed in the book's sub-title—can open youth work survive?—thus remains firmly on the agenda, especially given the practice's marginal status and limited political leverage. In part, this is because what limited new funding has been made available for 'youth services' since 2018 has often materialised only after long delays—if at all. Threats to its survival are the consequence too, however, of much of this money being targeted on tackling high-priority 'youth problems' rather than being explicitly and systematically committed to reinstating the full range of the local youth services' facilities—building-based and detached—lost since 2010.

Revealing here, too—as evidenced in Chap. 9—is that even when ministers have talked about improving young people's access to 'out of school activities', what they seem most often to assume is an armed services' cadet unit or a Scout or Guide group, DoE project—or even 'a sports team'. Missing from these statements and from government papers generally has been any recognition that in 2013 up to one million 8–25-year-olds were reported to be using their local youth club[4]—that is, a space where,

---

[2] Amrit Virdi, 2024, 'Labour Party manifesto: Boosting school-based support and votes for 16s among pledges', *CYPN*, 13 June; BBC News, 2024, 'Keir Starmer launches Labour Manifesto with wealth creation "number one priority"', https://www.bbc.co.uk/news/live/uk-politics-69111362; BBC News, 2024, 'Labour Manifesto: Take Back Our Streets', https://www.bbc.co.uk/news/live/uk-politics-69111362; https://labour.org.uk/change/take-back-our-streets/#antisocial-behaviour, accessed 13 June 2024.

[3] Larry Elliott, 2024, 'IMF warns Jeremy Hunt against tax cuts in budget', *Guardian*, 30 January; Phillip Inman, 2024, 'Jeremy Hunt's "dubious" financial planning lacks credibility, says IMF', *Guardian*, 27 February.

[4] National Council for Voluntary Youth Services, *Youth Report 2013*, NCYVS, file:///C:/Users/Owner/Favorites/Desktop/Documents/PolicyPapersetc%20-%20Copy/YouthSv'YthWk/NCVYSYthRpt2013.pdf, p. 2.

without any commitment in advance to joining a pre-set programme or scheme, they could, with their friends, engage with adults who, working through carefully negotiated trusting relationships, prioritised the interests and concerns which *they* brought with them.

Though at the grassroots strong practitioner commitments to these approaches remain, as we saw in Chap. 5, over the past decade both the government and influential organisations within the youth sector itself have broadened the meaning of 'youth work' to include practices and their providers whose starting points are often very different from—even at odds with—those of open youth work. As a result, even as open youth work providers have struggled to access resources, significant amounts of state funding have been 'invested' in the 'youth work' now on offer in, for example, youth offending projects, police stations, hospitals and schools.

In responding to the open youth work 'survival' question, therefore, this use of so many financial and other forms of state support needs to be named and then *confronted* for what it is—a diversion of vital resources and other support away from open youth work. However, two other issues explored in the book make this shift in analysis even more urgent, particularly for clarifying *how* to respond. One is the continuing impact on young people's lives of the pandemic and the cost-of-living crisis—pressures which, for the nearly half a million young people from vulnerable families unknown to other services,[5] may often now be being addressed only by what remains of the non-stigmatising practice of open youth work. The other is the need to commit more of whatever state and indeed philanthropic money is available to creating the 'small-scale, flexible and locally determined … pop-up or modular builds' recommended by the academics who responded to the DCMS's own Youth Review.[6]

Clearly, the relevance of these and indeed other proposals for open youth work and its delivery will require continuing critical debate and consultation within the sector, not least with young people themselves and with the face-to-face practitioners dealing with the on-the-ground dilemmas of implementing them. This, however, will need to be treated, not as an end in itself, but as the starting point for a sustained and forceful

[5] NYA, Between The Lines', March 2021, p. 4, https://static.nya.org.uk/static/f3fcc0c77f1f2d3b579af6274648540b/Between-the-lines-final-version.pdf.

[6] DCMS, 2022, *Youth Review: Summary findings and government response*, 1 February, p. 7, https://www.gov.uk/government/publications/youth-review-summary-findings-and-government-response/youth-review-summary-findings-and-government-response.

campaign focused unapologetically on the distinctiveness of open-access youth work practice and on the full restoration of its lost facilities.

Such a campaign will also—especially—need to emphasise the practice's potential for reaching and engaging significant numbers of often sceptical and hesitant young people, individually and in their peer groups. Indeed, the bottom line for such a campaign will need to be, as one young person vividly and bluntly reminded us in February 2023:

> Youth club used to be sick and then one day they just disappeared. There was bare youth clubs ... Young people don't have nothing ... they just want the kids to be on the streets now ....[7]

---

[7] Fiona Simpson, 2023, 'Youth work investment "key" to reducing exploitation over school holidays, Barnardo's says', *CYPN*, 2 June.

# Index[1]

[1] Note: Page numbers followed by 'n' refer to notes.

**SPRINGER NATURE**

# GPSR Compliance

*The European Union's (EU) General Product Safety Regulation (GPSR) is a set of rules that requires consumer products to be safe and our obligations to ensure this.*

*If you have any concerns about our products, you can contact us on ProductSafety@springernature.com*

In case Publisher is established outside the EU, the EU authorized representative is:

Springer Nature Customer Service Center GmbH
Europaplatz 3
69115 Heidelberg, Germany

The manufacturer's authorised representative in the EU is Springer Nature Customer Service Centre GmbH, Europaplatz 3, 69115 Heidelberg, Germany. If you have any concerns regarding our products, please contact ProductSafety@springernature.com

Printed and bound by CPI Group (UK) Ltd, Croydon, CR0 4YY
24/04/2026
02096368-0002